pure erotic massage

NICOLE BAILEY

pure erotic massage

TOUCH FEEL AROUSE

DUNCAN BAIRD PUBLISHERS

LONDON

PURE EROTIC MASSAGE

NICOLE BAILEY

Distributed in the USA and Canada by Sterling Publishing Co., Inc.
387 Park Avenue South, New York, NY 10016-8810

This edition first published in the UK and USA in 2007 by Duncan Baird Publishers Ltd
Sixth Floor, Castle House, 75–76 Wells Street, London W1T 3QH

Conceived, created and designed by Duncan Baird Publishers
Copyright © Duncan Baird Publishers 2007
Text copyright © Kesta Desmond (writing as Nicole Bailey) 2007
Photography copyright © Duncan Baird Publishers 2007

Managing Editor: Grace Cheetham
Editor: Dawn Bates
Managing Designer: Manisha Patel
Designer: Jantje Doughty
Photographer: John Davis

Library of Congress Cataloging-in-Publication Data Available
ISBN-13: 978-1-84483-480-8
ISBN-10: 1-84483-480-8
10 9 8 7 6 5 4 3 2 1

Typeset in Gill Sans
Color reproduction by Colourscan, Singapore
Printed in Singapore by Imago

For information about custom editions, special sales, premium and corporate purchases, please
contact Sterling Special Sales Department at 800-805-5489 or specialsales@sterlingpub.com.

PUBLISHERS' NOTE: The information in this book is not intended as a substitute for
professional medical advice and treatment. If you are pregnant or are suffering from any medical conditions or health problems, it is recommended that you consult a medical professional
before following any of the advice or practice suggested in this book. Duncan Baird Publishers, or
any other persons who have been involved in working on this publication, cannot accept responsibility for any injuries or damage incurred as a result of following the information, exercises, or
therapeutic techniques contained in this book. Do not use massage oil if you are using a condom
—the oil damages latex.

contents

introduction

One of the greatest sensual pleasures in life comes from exploring a lover's body through touch. This happens naturally during that blissful honeymoon period at the start of a relationship. You just can't keep your hands off one another. And nothing feels more important than spending entire days in bed discovering what makes each other tick sexually. But when the relationship settles down and the honeymoon period is over it's easy to get out of the habit of touching in ways that truly connect you to one another. This is why erotic massage is so wonderful – it brings passion, playfulness, connection, eroticism and sensuality.

ANYONE CAN DO IT!

Anyone can deliver erotic pleasure through massage. You don't need to attend classes, you don't need to learn complicated strokes or techniques – you just need to tune in to the sensual power that lies in your palms and fingertips. In fact, it doesn't even have to be in your hands – you can deliver a sublime massage using your lips, your tongue, your hair or even your toes. A massage can take all day or it can be as quick and simple as stroking your lover's face and neck before you go to sleep.

MAKE LOVE WITH YOUR WHOLE BODY

The aim of this book is to help you to turn sex from a mainly genital experience into a whole-body experience. Slowing down your approach to sex and using touch to explore your lover's body in its entirety can lead to all kinds of discoveries. You may find new erogenous zones; you may find that you can take your arousal levels to new heights; you may discover greater trust and intimacy with your lover. Or you may simply find that sex is more playful, fun and creative when you take the time to explore. Massage is good for all sorts of things too: it can help you "stay in touch" when you're not in the mood for intercourse (it's great during pregnancy or the first few months of parenthood when you may simply be too tired for sex); it's a good way to reconnect with each other if you've been physically or emotionally apart; and it's also a great way of being generous and giving your lover "a gift".

HOW TO USE THIS BOOK

This is a great book to read with a lover – let the erotic photography inspire you and take it in turns to choose a particular massage or exercise.

If sensual touch has slipped down the list of priorities in your relationship, dedicate one night per week to erotic touch. Light some candles, undress each other and then open this book at random and see where it takes you! If you've recently met your lover, use the book to enhance your discovery of each other.

FROM SENSUAL TOUCH TO SELF-TOUCH
There are five chapters in the book – each one describes a different type of touch with different levels of eroticism. In chapter one, Sensual Touch, I explain how to give and receive the kinds of touch and massage that give you both wonderful whole-body melting or floating sensations. This is a great starting point for getting more sexy and intimate.

Once you've put your lover into a heightened sensual state, they'll be more than open and ready for the erotic touch techniques in chapter two. This chapter not only tells you how to massage the erotic hot spots of the body – the breasts, penis, clitoris and G-spot – it also explains how to seduce your lover with erotic fantasy and give a sexy massage using your mouth.

To turn the sexual temperature up even higher, chapter three, Sex Touch, shows you how you can massage your lover and yourself during lovemaking. The combination of trying out sensual touch techniques while experimenting with a range of sex positions, including some from Eastern texts the *Kama Sutra* and *Ananga Ranga,* will take you and your lover to new heights of pleasure and revitalize your lovemaking.

In Tantric Touch, the fourth chapter, I show you how you can work toward a deep sense of trust, union and bliss with your lover by using the techniques of Tantric touch. These bring harmony and sensuality and create a new level of intimacy between you and your lover.

Touching and being touched is all the more pleasurable if you are at one with your body and know what feels good. There's no better way to discover this than through sensual self-touch. So in chapter five, I explain how you can get into a sensual or eroticized state all by yourself.

Erotic massage is a wonderful way to communicate how you feel about your lover and to give to each other. I hope by using this book you and your lover will experience a new openness in your lovemaking. Enjoy your journey of sensual touch...

CHAPTER ONE

SENSUAL TOUCH

To take your lover to the heights of sensual bliss all you need are your hands, a bottle of massage oil and plenty of time. This chapter takes you through the core massage strokes and shows you how to apply them to your lover's body. Learn how to benefit from sensual touch by fully immersing yourself in the experience when giving and receiving a massage. Get these basics right and every touch will make your lover tingle with pleasure.

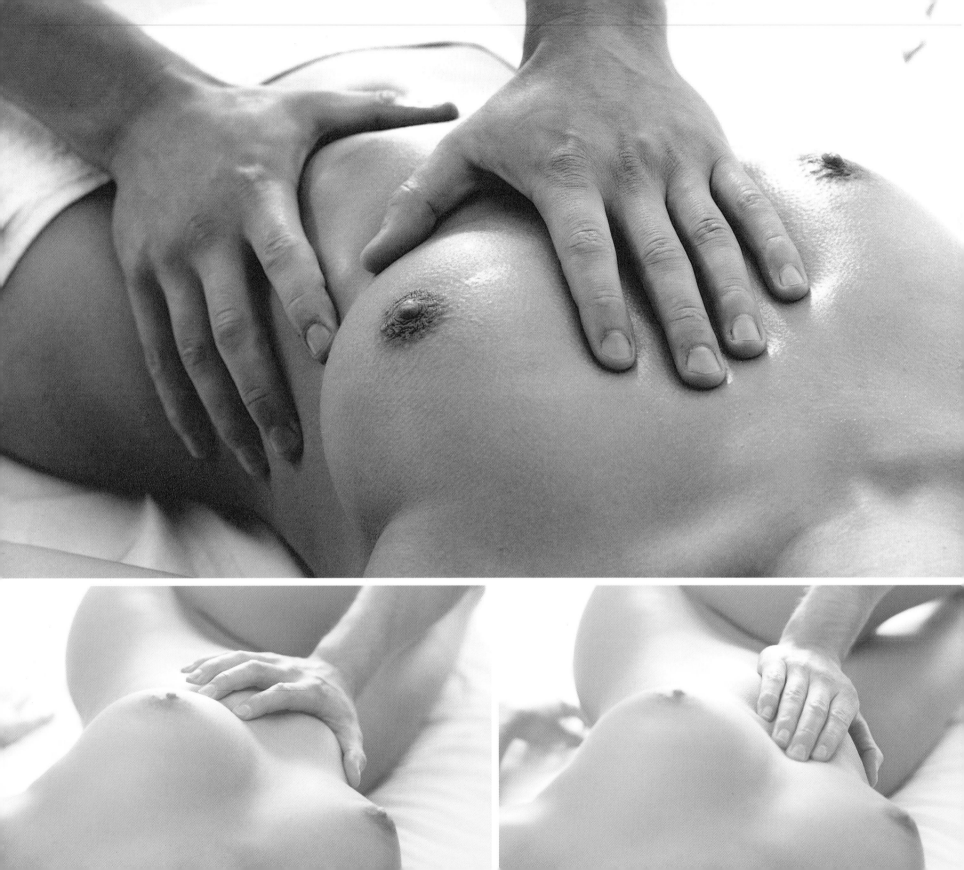

basic sensual touch techniques

To begin incorporating sensual touch into your lovemaking, it can help to familiarize yourself with some basic massage techniques. These create a range of wonderful sensations that are both relaxing and stimulating. You don't have to learn each massage stroke by heart or use all of them in one session – just one or two simple techniques applied in a loving and attentive way can feel sublime.

GLIDING

Lay your hands flat on your lover's body and move them smoothly across the skin (see left), using firm or light pressure. Plenty of massage oil will create a lovely, slippery feeling – if your hands drag, you need to use more oil. Gliding strokes are good for putting your lover at ease and for lubricating the skin. They are also a good way of letting your hands travel from one part of your lover's body to another.

KNEADING

Choose a fleshy part of your lover's body and squeeze it between your fingers and thumbs. As one hand lifts off, your other hand should begin the next stroke. This way your hands are always in contact with the skin. Kneading is a firm stroke that releases tension from the body and is good for making your lover feel relaxed and tingly.

TAPPING

Curl your hands into loose fists and using the side or the flat part of the middle of your fingers – not your knuckles – tap your lover's legs, shoulders or back. Keep your movements fairly fast and rhythmic, and your wrists loose and relaxed. Tapping, also known as percussing, can be both energizing and relaxing.

THUMB PRESSURE

Use the pads of your thumbs to apply static pressure or to make small circular movements. If you want to increase the pressure, lean your body weight into your thumbs, rather than just pressing harder. Thumb pressure releases knots of tension found in muscular areas, such as the upper back. Just before you lift one thumb, bring the other thumb down behind it so your hands don't break contact with your lover's body.

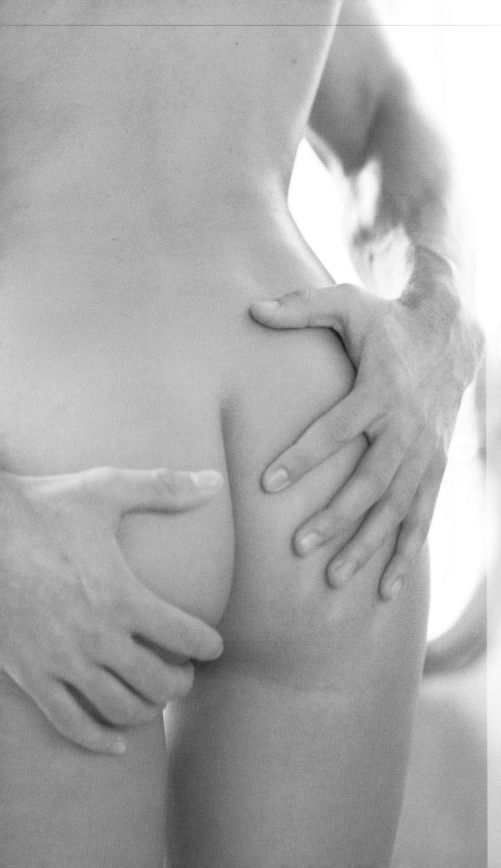

PRESSING

As well as applying pressure with your thumbs, you can press with your palms, fingertips, heels of your hands, fists (the flat part at the top of your fists), forearms or elbows. Pressing strokes are good for releasing muscle tension and helping someone to relax. Apply pressure gradually by leaning your body weight forward into your hand. Avoid pressing on delicate areas of the body or on the spine. Ask for feedback.

Pressure can be static or circular. If you are using your fists, you can twist them in a single spot. Fingertip pressure is good for giving your lover a face massage. Forearm pressure feels wonderful on the back. Hand pressure (see left) is particularly effective on muscular areas, such as the buttocks, and can be very pleasurable and stimulating for both of you. It can also be applied in rolling movements – start by pressing through the heel of your hand and then roll your hand forward to apply pressure through your palm and then your fingers and fingertips.

RAKING

Rest your fingertips on your lover's body and rake them across the skin. This stroke creates a wealth of different sensations, depending on how fast you do it and how hard you press: fast and hard is arousing and energizing; soft and slow is delicious and sensual. Hard raking works best on muscular areas, such as the back and buttocks. Soft raking is needed for more delicate areas, such as the breasts and belly.

One of the most seductive touches is when the fingertips barely brush the surface of the skin. If you have long fingernails, you can create delicious sensations on your lover's body by using them to gently graze the skin (see above right) – this feels wonderful on the neck, chest or flanks. Just before you lift one hand off the skin, begin raking with the other. To vary raking, turn your hand over and stroke your lover's body with the backs of your fingers or the flats of your nails. This is a gentle and loving stroke and it is great to use on the arms, legs, neck and face.

KNUCKLING

Make your hands into fists and rest your knuckles on your lover's body. Now roll your knuckles from side to side, applying pressure as you go (see below right). This feels great on the back, shoulders and the palms and is an effective way to relieve muscle tension. Be gentle, though – knuckling can hurt if you press too hard, especially on a sensitive or a bony part of the body. Never put pressure directly on the spine. Always ask your lover for feedback and adapt the pressure or stroke you're using if necessary.

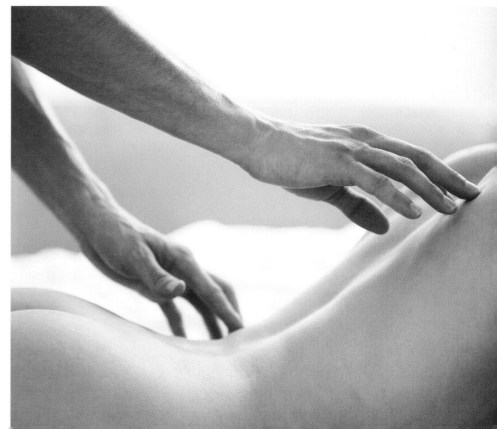

enhance the massage experience

MAKING MASSAGE OIL

Essential oils are concentrated plant essences which must be diluted in a carrier oil before being applied to the skin. There is a variety of different carrier oils available – for example, almond, grapeseed, soya or apricot kernel – so choose your lover's favourite. For a particularly arousing and sensual scent, opt for patchouli, ylang ylang or jasmine.

If your lover has dry skin, choose a heavier, stickier carrier oil, such as avocado, olive, jojoba or wheatgerm oil.

To make your own oil, simply add 20 drops of an essential oil to 50 ml (2 fl oz) of a carrier oil. Then put it in a dark-coloured, watertight container and shake it well. It will keep for 6–12 months.

To put the techniques you've learned into practice, think about the environment in which you're massaging and do all that you can to make sure your lover is comfortable and relaxed.

Create a calming, intimate atmosphere in the room by dimming the lights, lighting candles, burning incense or essential oils, and playing soft, meditative music. If it's cold, turn the heating up. Warm some towels on a radiator and use them to cover the lower half of your lover's body. Don't forget to make sure your hands are warm too.

Oil is an important ingredient in a sensual massage – it can stimulate the senses and create an overall more sensual experience for both of you. There are plenty of ready-made massage oils available, but it's easy to make your own by combining an essential oil with a carrier oil (see left).

Warm the oil before you apply it: rub it between your hands or, if you are using a bottle of oil, let it rest in a bowl of hot water first. If you are giving a genital massage (see pages 50–3) and are planning to make love afterwards using a condom, use a water-based lubricant instead – oil can damage the latex and make the condom less effective.

discover the beauty of touch

The experience of giving someone a massage can be greatly enhanced if you think about what it really means to touch someone. Massage demands a high degree of sensitivity from your fingers and hands – something that you may not have cultivated until now. The following exercise can help you to build or re-awaken the sensitivity in your hands and fingers – by depriving you of your other senses, it allows you to use only your sense of touch.

EXPLORING OBJECTS

Ask your lover to collect ten objects that give a variety of tactile sensations. Here are some ideas: a smooth pebble, a bowl of sand, a rubber glove, a ball of plasticine, an open tub of hand cream, a slice of melon, a metal comb, a piece of chocolate, screwed-up paper and a flower. Now sit down at a table and put on a blindfold. Ask your lover to place the objects in front of you one at a time. Pick up each object gently and reverentially – as if it had the potential to be fragile or precious – and explore it with your fingertips, investigating every crack, ripple, curve or crevice. Don't use any other sense to explore the object – don't smell or taste it, even if you're pretty sure it's food. Try to mentally describe the object in terms of its texture, rather than rushing to identify it in words. Is it hard or soft, fragile or strong, pliable or resilient, smooth or rough, cool or warm, wet or dry, heavy or light? Does it have corners, edges, dimples? Is it solid or fluid? Meditate upon the object through your sense of touch. Even when you think you know what the object is, carry on exploring it anyway. Imagine that you have never touched this object before and that you are trying to memorize it using your fingers.

When you have finished exploring, take off your blindfold and look at all ten objects. Ask yourself whether your exploration was richer because you used only your sense of touch. Now collect ten items for your lover and repeat the experiment.

THE TEXTURE OF THE BODY

While the experience of this touch experiment is still fresh in your mind, sit on the floor or bed and put on a blindfold. Ask your lover to lie down beside you. Now gently lower your hands onto any part of your lover's body and let them rest there. Don't try to direct your hands to

an obvious erogenous zone, such as the breasts or genitals – just allow them to land randomly. Even if you immediately identify the part of your lover's body you are touching, try not to make this the focus of your attention. Instead, use your hands as if they were your only means of sensing the world. Let them remain still for a while, soaking up sensations from your lover's skin. Then slowly and gently begin to explore the area you are touching. What can you feel? Is this part of your lover's body warm or cool, soft or hard, hairy or smooth, dry or damp? Can you sense any tension in this part of the body?

Note whether your hands know intuitively how to touch this part of your lover's body. Does this area need to be gently stroked and caressed or does it need to be firmly pressed and kneaded? If you feel the urge to touch your lover in a particular way, go ahead. Sometimes you may feel inclined to simply let your hands rest motionless and allow your energy to pass into your lover. Try touching different parts of your lover in this way. After the session, ask for feedback to gauge how in tune you were with these touch sensations. Then swap positions and let your lover do the same to you.

how to give a massage

You can master all the massage strokes in the world, but your lover won't enjoy receiving them if he or she senses you are in some way holding back and not enjoying the experience too. Giving someone a massage should be a pleasure and not a chore.

If you make yourself comfortable, centre yourself and really connect with your lover, you can enter a sensual, blissful state in unison and get as much pleasure from giving as you would from receiving.

CENTRE YOURSELF

Before giving a massage, take a few minutes to ground and centre yourself so that you can focus fully on your lover and shut out any distracting noises or thoughts.

Sit on the floor of your massage space in a crossed-leg position with your spine straight. Ask your lover to lie down and relax while you do this. Close your eyes and bring your attention to your breath – keep focusing on the ebb and flow of air. Gradually bring your breath deeper inside your body so your belly moves out on each inhalation and in on each exhalation.

Spend a few minutes focusing on these deep belly breaths. Now try to concentrate on all the warm, loving, compassionate feelings you have for your lover. When you feel ready, open your eyes and gaze at your lover. Relish the time you are about to share.

ASK PERMISSION

You may feel that if you've planned to massage your lover and they are lying there waiting for your touch, their permission has already been given. Yet the formality of asking for permission makes the massage into something special – a ritual that has a clear beginning. It also helps your lover to feel empowered and in control.

This is especially important if you are touching parts of your lover's body that they feel sensitive or self-conscious about. Also, by asking permission, you are showing respect for your lover's body and communicating the idea that you won't do anything that they don't want you to do. You can ask for permission in whatever way feels natural. For example: "May I put my hands on you?" or simply "Are you ready for me to touch you?"

SYNCHRONIZE BREATHING

When you put your hands on your lover's body, keep them still at first and sense the rise and fall of their breath through your palms. Close your eyes and try to match your inhalations and exhalations to theirs so that you are at one with each other.

If your lover's breathing is fast and shallow, start by taking fast and shallow breaths yourself, then gradually make your breath slower and deeper – their breath will follow yours. Breathing in synchrony allows you to stay connected and to relax in harmony with each other. At various points during the massage, check that your breath is still synchronized with your lover's.

MAKE YOURSELF COMFORTABLE

It is essential that you feel comfortable throughout the massage. If you are feeling tense or uncomfortable, not only will you not enjoy the massage, but you'll transmit your tension to your lover and may have to cut the session short. You also need to make sure you are wearing the right clothes so that you're not too hot or cold. Check that your posture is not twisted and that you are not leaning over your lover at a difficult angle. If you are on the floor, kneel on something soft, such as a towel or a duvet. If your arms or hands begin to ache, use a less penetrating massage stroke for a while.

HANDS ON

It may sound like a small detail, but keeping your hands in contact with your lover's body for the duration of a massage is very important. If your lover is in a deeply relaxed state, breaking contact can break the feeling of relaxation and the connection between the two of you. If you need to move your hands from one end of your lover's body to another, use a gliding stroke (see page 13) to stay in contact.

ASK FOR FEEDBACK

It's important to feel confident that your lover is enjoying the massage, so ask for feedback throughout the massage. This might be a satisfied "Mmmm", or single words such as "Nice", "More" or "Harder". If your lover doesn't like something you're doing, ask what they would prefer. The more feedback you get, the more pleasure you will give – and this will make the whole experience more satisfying for you.

DON'T TALK

Beyond asking for occasional feedback, don't talk, and don't encourage your lover to talk. Talking encourages thinking, and during the massage you should both exist solely in the realm of your senses.

STAY IN THE MOMENT

You won't give a good massage if your thoughts are elsewhere. Try to tune into your lover and simply think about the pleasure you are giving. Let go of any other thoughts and distractions. If this is difficult, try concentrating on your breathing, or try to imagine that you are the person receiving the sensations you are creating with your hands. If you're playing soft music, you may want to tune into that.

MAXIMIZE THE MOOD

When you've finished massaging your lover, don't get up straight away. Stay with the mood of intimacy and connection that you've created. Try these suggestions: lie in the spoons position (see page 100) with your lover and concentrate on breathing together; lie face to face and gaze into each other's eyes or embrace and caress each other and let the relaxed, sensual mood slowly build into something more erotic.

how to receive a massage

To get something out of being massaged, you need to put something in. If you can give yourself up to the physical feeling and make it clear how you enjoy being touched, you'll experience a far greater range of sensations.

CLEARING YOUR MIND

A common way in which people sabotage the pleasure of a massage is to be preoccupied with thoughts. You might be thinking about something you were doing earlier or jobs you need to do later; or you may be distracted by something that is worrying you. It's also common to take away from the experience by thinking about the massage itself. For example, you might be worried that your lover is looking at your body in a critical way or is bored with giving the massage. You might be thinking about the fact that you want the massage to lead to sex. All of these thoughts, and a hundred others, can take you away from your senses and dull you to the feelings that are present in your body.

One of the simplest ways of stilling your mind is to bring your attention to your breath. As you inhale, imagine you are taking your breath directly to the area being massaged. Feel the intake of breath as a sensual act in itself. Imagine your breath caressing the inside of your body in the same way that your lover's hands are caressing the outside. As you exhale, imagine tension floating out of your body and taking all thoughts and distractions with it. While you are receiving a massage keep two words in mind: trust and surrender. Trust your lover to touch you in a caring way and in a spirit of generosity. Surrender your body and mind by letting go of your defences and inhibitions.

ENJOYING THE MASSAGE

If the way your lover is touching you feels uncomfortable or painful, there is an art to letting them know. Instead of criticizing, which will only de-motivate – give specific information about how you want to be touched. For example, say "Softer" instead of "You're pressing too hard," or "Can you move your hand slightly lower?" instead of " Don't massage me there." The time for giving detailed feedback is when the massage has finished. Even then, try to emphasize the positive rather than the negative. And be specific – for example, say "I loved it when you ran your fingers through my hair and all the way down my back."

touch me there...

You can never know too much about what turns you both on. Although you may have discussed what you like sexually, you may not have talked about what you want in terms of sensual touch – the kind of touch that makes you shiver and tingle, or creates a feeling of relaxed, trance-like bliss. It's fun and arousing to sit down with your lover and create a touch wish list. If you're too embarrassed or shy to tell your lover where you want to be touched, make a game of it by letting them explore your body and rating your favourite zones from one to ten.

HOT SPOTS

Take turns to tell each other where you would most like to be massaged or caressed. Remember, the aim is sensuality rather than orgasm. Create a top five or a top ten list of your favourite erogenous zones. Lots of people love receiving a head, back or foot massage, but you don't have to stick to predictable requests. Unconventional zones might be behind your knees, in your armpits, along the line of your collar bone, on your wrists, or on your fingertips. If there are parts of your body where you don't like to be touched, tell your lover about these too. Feeling uncomfortable about being touched in a particular place doesn't necessarily mean that your lover should never touch you there, but it's important that they are aware of and sensitive about these places.

TOUCH TYPES

Give detailed information about the types of touch you most enjoy. For example, do you love deep, penetrating pressure and feel tickled by anything lighter? Do you like the feeling of being gently stroked and caressed? Does the type of touch you want change according to your mood or how relaxed you are feeling? Do you like different types of touch on different parts of your body?

Be as specific as you can. For example, say "I would really love you to tweak my earlobes, pummel my shoulders and back, stroke my belly with the palm of your hand, press your fists into my buttocks, and make shampooing movements with your fingers all over my scalp." Listen carefully when your lover tells you how they like to be touched – it's easy to make assumptions, but a detailed guide from them is the only way you'll truly know what they enjoy.

sensual awakening

Now that you've both thought about how you want to give and receive massage, try putting it into practice with this sensual awakening exercise. Give each other feedback afterwards and adapt it to suit yourselves.

IS IT FOR ME?

The heady delights of exploring every millimetre of each other when you're at the beginning of your relationship can fade over time. If you've been together quite a while, you may find that the way you touch each other consists of kissing hello or goodbye, cuddling in bed or stimulating each other's genitals or breasts during sex. Although these all feel great, you can enhance the physical and emotional connection between the two of you by incorporating the whole of your body into lovemaking.

The sensual awakening exercise consists of four stages. The first stage is about getting back to the basics of touch, and the stages that follow are about progressively enhancing sensuality. You can do each part immediately after each other, or on separate days or weeks. This exercise will be hugely beneficial if any of the following statements are true for you and your lover:

- You can't remember when you last touched your lover's body anywhere except for the obvious hot spots, such as the breasts and genitals.
- You're finding it increasingly difficult to get aroused by each other – sex has started to feel perfunctory.
- The physical sensations you experience during sex lack intensity.
- You have trouble getting an erection or reaching orgasm.
- You want to feel closer and more connected when you have sex.
- You rarely have sex or cuddle or touch each other.

ABSTAINING FROM SEX

It's recommended that you avoid having sex during the days or weeks when you are trying the sensual massage programme. This might seem odd given that one of the aims of the programme is to enhance sexual connection, but it's crucial to its success. The reason is that abstaining from sex encourages you to think about touch in its simplest form and helps you break away from ingrained, habitual ways of touching and making love. It also takes away all of the potential performance pressure of orgasm or penetration (this is especially helpful if you are having trouble with these areas of your lovemaking). This in turn frees you up to be more experimental and playful.

Although sensual awakening is a fantastic way to re-connect with your lover and overcome any sexual difficulties, do seek professional help from a counsellor or sex therapist if you have serious or entrenched sexual or emotional problems. Also, if you have problems getting an erection or reaching orgasm, there may be an underlying medical reason – consult a doctor to eliminate this possibility.

TAKE AWAY TIME PRESSURES

It is essential that you allocate sufficient time to carry out this sensual massage programme – it is not possible to achieve deep sensuality and relaxation to a deadline. Try to dedicate several hours, or an entire morning, afternoon or evening if you can, to each stage of the programme. If you have a whole day, this is even better and, as well as massaging each other, you can spend time reconnecting by talking, going for walks, listening to music and cooking for each other. Make sure you won't be interrupted during any stage.

STAGE 1

Explore your lover's body through touch. As well as using the basic techniques (see pages 12–15), trace the outline of your lover's face with your fingertip, walking your fingers up their thighs, rolling their fingers between your thumb and forefinger. Experiment with different speeds and pressures. During this stage of the programme avoid touching your lover's breasts or genitals – this will help you focus on sensuality rather than eroticism.

STAGE 2

Repeat stage 1, but include your lover's breasts and genitals. Your aim is not to bring your lover to orgasm, but to give them a sensual experience that encompasses their whole body. Touch their genitals and breasts in a playful, exploratory way rather than in a way that is familiar, and don't give these areas more attention than the rest of the body.

STAGE 3

Now take it in turns to massage each other. As in the previous stages, rather than trying to reach orgasm you're aiming to awaken a new level of sensitivity in each other's body and give each other delicious sensations. Use as much oil as you want, and experiment with props

– a silk scarf, a piece of velvet, a soft paintbrush or hairbrush. You don't have to do anything complicated with these objects. Simply sitting behind your lover and brushing their hair in long, smooth strokes, or wafting a silk scarf over their naked skin can be a sensational experience.

STAGE 4

Now you can touch each other at the same time, using oil and props and including the breasts and genitals. This mutual touching takes sensuality and eroticism to the next level because you can both feed off each other's responses. As tempting as it might be to have sex or stimulate each other to orgasm, try to resist. Concentrate on the pleasurable feelings without getting carried away by them. Practise this stage three times. You can now return to having sex and climaxing.

USING WHAT YOU'VE LEARNED

After doing this exercise, describe what you enjoyed and the sensations you felt. Try to maintain and use what you've learned from each stage before and during your lovemaking. The following pages outline simple step-by-step massage techniques for the head, back and feet that you can use as part of the sensual awakening exercise.

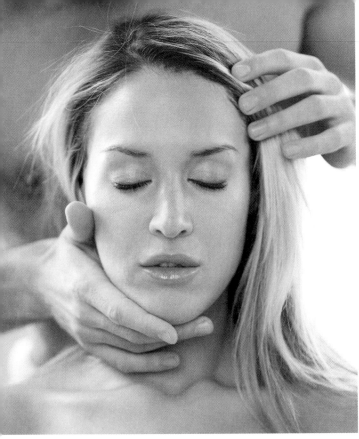

sensual head massage

A head massage is a sensual, soothing and extremely comforting form of massage. It's a wonderfully quick and effective way of making tension just melt away. It's also a great way to nurture each other and create a mood of relaxed, loving intimacy. Head massage is traditional in India where it is known as *champi* or *champissage*.

STEP 1 (see above left) **Ask your lover to sit in a straight-backed chair and close their eyes. Gently place your hands on their shoulders. Take three deep breaths in synchrony with each other. Then gently caress your lover's face with your fingertips – on their forehead, chin and along the cheekbones.**

STEP 2 (see below left) **Coat your hands in oil (coconut oil is a traditional choice for massaging the head) and rake your fingers through your lover's hair using long, smooth strokes. Apply light pressure with your fingertips throughout (imagine your fingertips are the teeth of a wide-toothed comb). Repeat this step for several minutes to relax your lover fully.**

STEP 3 **Support the forehead with the palm of one hand and gently press the heel of your other hand into the curve where their neck joins the base of their skull. Slowly roll this hand so that you apply pressure through your palm, then your fingers and then your fingertips. Move your hand up and repeat the stroke on the top of the head.**

STEP 4 (see left) **Place your fingertips above your lover's ears and apply gentle pressure while moving them in slow circles. Repeat this stroke on your lover's temples. If you prefer, you can use the heels of your hands.**

STEP 5 **Place your fingertips and thumbs widely apart on your lover's head. Draw them together in a pinching movement, then spread them out again. Repeat this shampooing movement all over the scalp.**

STEP 6 **Gather sections of hair in your hands, starting at the top and working in strips down the head. Gently tug each section. Finally, use the tips of your fingers to tap your lover's scalp all over. Keep your fingers floppy and use fast and light movements.**

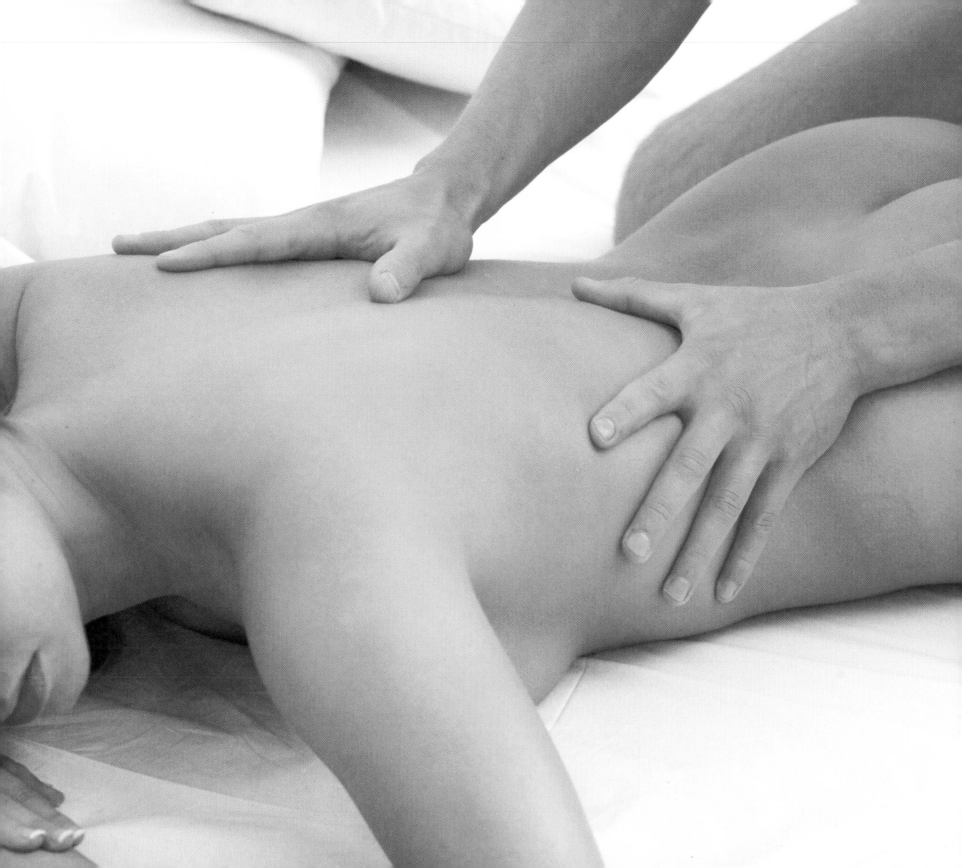

sensual back massage

A simple back massage can lift your lover into a realm of pure sensual bliss and relaxation. It is a wonderful way to build up to sex gradually. Use plenty of base oil, such as almond or olive oil, so that your hands glide effortlessly over the skin. If you like, you can also add a few drops of a sweet and sensual essential oil, such as rose or jasmine.

STEP 1 (see left) **Ask your lover to lie on their front and kneel astride them. Place your hands on the base of the back, one hand on either side of the spine. Lean forward to transfer your body weight into your hands. When you're applying a comfortable amount of pressure, stay still for 30 seconds and then slide your hands up the length of their back.**

STEP 2 (see right) **When you reach the top of their back, gently glide your hands across the shoulders and then diagonally back to the starting position. Repeat steps 1 and 2.**

STEP 3 **Make your hands into fists and place the flat part (see page 15) on the upper back. Don't massage directly on to the spine. Transfer a little body weight into your fists and twist them. Now apply firm pressure with your thumbs on the upper back muscles.**

STEP 4 **Repeat step 1, but now, each time your hands come back to the base of the back, slightly reduce the pressure. Eventually, just stroke your lover gently using your fingertips and then your fingernails only.**

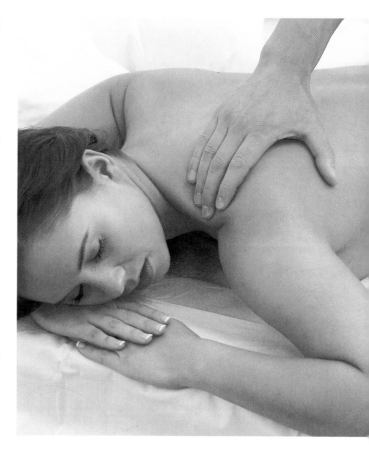

sensual foot massage

The foot is a major erogenous zone for many people. Spend time giving undivided attention to your lover's feet. Wash them, dry them and then indulge them with this exquisite massage.

STEP I **Ask your lover to sit or lie down and then sandwich their foot in between your warm, oiled hands. Hold it securely for a minute and then stroke both your hands along its length. Next hold the heel in one hand and the toes in the other. Move your lover's foot in slow circles, both clockwise and anti-clockwise.**

STEP 2 (see above right) **Rest your fingertips on the top of your lover's foot and position your thumbs on the sole. Now press in tiny circular movements. Do this in the same place for about a minute and then repeat along the length of the foot.**

STEP 3 (see below right) **Hold the heel of your lover's foot in one hand and, using the thumb of your other hand, press firmly all the way along the underside of the foot. Do this several times.**

STEP 4 **Using your thumb and fingers, squeeze and rotate each toe in turn, moving from the base of the toe to the tip. When you reach the tip, gently pull on the toe.**

STEP 5 **Hold your lover's toes in one hand and use the thumb of your other hand to press the sole of the foot. Imagine that there are five lines – each one begins at the base of**

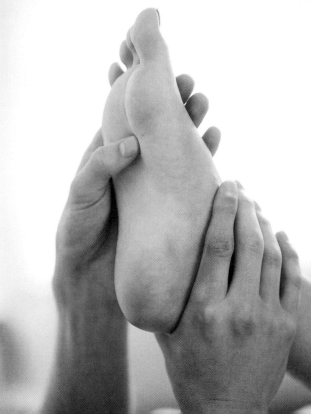

each toe and finishes at the heel. Apply firm pressure along each of these lines.

STEP 6 **Support your lover's heel in one hand. Rest the heel of your other hand on the underside of their toes and apply pressure – the aim is to give the toes an invigorating backward stretch. Now use the palm of your hand to pull the toes back the other way (towards the underside of the foot).**

STEP 7 (see left) **Finish by rotating each foot in circular movements, clockwise and anti-clockwise, around their ankle. Then press their foot firmly between your hands.**

STEP 8 **When you have finished the massage, gently enclose your lover's foot in a warm towel. Then massage the other foot, repeating steps 1–8.**

There's no better way to start the day than with this massage treat designed to gradually awaken and arouse your lover. And it's a particularly good start to the weekend. Begin by slipping your hands under the covers and sliding your palms in long, gentle but confident movements along the length of their body. Apply a little more pressure to muscular areas such as the back and thighs, and a little less to sensitive areas such as the belly and groin. Tantalize your lover by letting your fingertips play at their breasts and genitals.

Following this gentle warm-up, kiss your lover on the lips and ask them to lie on their back and remove any items of clothing. Pour some sensual massage oil into your hands and kneel astride your lover. Place your hands on their belly, then let them gently glide up to their chest and back down along their side, using a soft raking technique (see pages 14 – 15). Repeat this stroke as many times as you like.

Now ask your lover to roll over and apply smooth, gliding strokes (see page 13) along the length of their back from the base of the spine to the shoulders and back again. Vary the strokes by continuing up along the neck and applying fingertip pressure to the scalp. Finally, use the sides of your hands in a hacking motion over their shoulders. Once your lover is fully awake, what happens next is entirely up to you!

CHAPTER TWO

EROTIC TOUCH

Get down – quite literally – to the basics of erotic massage. Learn how to massage the hottest spots on your lover's body from the G-spot – or P-spot – to the clitoris and frenulum. Discover how to ramp up your lover's arousal levels by using your penis or vagina as a massage tool – no hands required. It's guaranteed that foreplay will never be the same again!

what turns your lover on?

In chapter one you learned to be more open about touch and more relaxed about touching each other. Now, as you up the eroticism, it's time to get down to the nitty gritty of what really turns your lover on! Some couples make love together for years without knowing, for example, that her favourite way to receive oral sex is in the 69 position or that he loves having his penis caressed slowly and gently instead of fast and furiously.

ASKING QUESTIONS

The following exercise is a no-holds-barred way of really discovering what your lover needs and wants. Start by reading the questions aloud and taking it in turns to answer.

• Do you enjoy receiving massage?

• What was your first experience of erotic touch?

• How do you rate your sensitivity to touch on a scale of one to ten?

• Do you respond quickly to being touched and massaged or does it take you a while to relax into your body and experience pleasure?

• Does anything block you from enjoying touch and massage?

• Do you enjoy giving a massage?

• Is there enough touch and massage in our relationship?

• What's the most erotic way in which I've touched you?

• What would more touch and massage bring to our relationship?

• Would you like more erotic touch and massage as part of the build-up to sex?

• Would you like to give or receive massage during sex?

• Would you sometimes enjoy having an erotic massage as an alternative to sex?

• Which types of touch make you feel relaxed and sensual?

If asking questions feels too clinical, make a game of it. Pretend that you are a couple of virgins learning how to touch each other for the first time, or that the person doing the interview is a sex therapist. Role play is a fun way to free yourself from embarrassment and inhibition.

THE TIME

Ask your lover at what time of the day they feel most sexy. Some of us are morning people; some of us are night people. If your lover hates mornings, and an erotic wake-up call (see pages 38–9) is never going to work, this is valuable information. Women are sometimes affected by their menstrual cycle; some are very easily aroused at the midpoint of their cycle when they ovulate, while others get turned on just before or during their period. Women: if you're not sure when your sex drive peaks, keep a diary for two or three menstrual cycles (or longer). Make a note of the times you notice an increase in sexy thoughts, fantasies or dreams; when you masturbate most; when sexual sensation is at its height; or when you most want sex with your lover.

THE PLACE

Ask your lover exactly where on their body they like to be touched and then quiz them about the details. Don't make any assumptions. Ask her where she likes to be touched on her clitoris (for example, directly on the tip, on the clitoral hood, or above the clitoris; to the left or the right). Ask him where he likes to be touched on his penis (for example, on the base of the shaft, the middle or top of the shaft, or the glans; or all over). Ask equally detailed questions about the testicles,

the perineum, the vagina, the G-spot, the breasts and nipples, and the buttocks. Plus any other erotic zones you or your lover can think of!

THE PRESSURE AND SPEED

Ask your lover what sort of pressure and speed of touch they like on each different erotic zone. If, for example, your lover likes slow, gentle strokes on the shaft of his penis, ask him when or whether he likes those strokes to get faster and harder. If she loves G-spot massage, ask her how much pressure feels good and whether static pressure feels more enjoyable than movement. Ask your lover to use number ratings from one to five to describe the amount of pressure they like. One means the fingertips just brush the skin. Five means deep, penetrating pressure. Gather information about the variety of techniques your lover enjoys – the same sort of touch every time can be de-sensitizing.

THE POSITION

What position does your lover like to be in while being touched or massaged? Some people find it the height of eroticism to receive a genital massage or oral sex while they are standing up, whereas others like to be fully relaxed and lying down. And is there a position that your lover likes you to be in? He might, for example, be turned on by you kneeling with your back to him while you're giving him oral sex so that he gets a good view of your buttocks.

SPECIAL PLEASURES

Most people have fantasy sex scenarios – swap fantasies by disclosing one yourself and then asking for one back from your lover. Here are some experiences that people might fantasize about: being touched in secret while you are both out in public (touching each other under a table in a restaurant, for example); being tied up and then touched and teased; experimenting with different touch sensations by using sex toys; trying a new form of massage, such as anal massage; receiving a massage from two people at the same time.

GETTING HOTTER

Having done your erotic touch interview, try putting what you've discovered into practice. Give your lover a massage and ask them to give you feedback using the "getting hotter" exercise. This involves them

rating your touch in terms of eroticism by whispering the words: "Cool" (nothing erotic going on), "Warm" (it's starting to feel sexy), or "Hot" (the peak of eroticism). Although your lover's facial expression and body language can give you clues about what they're feeling, words tell you instantly when you're doing something exactly right.

OVERCOMING BLOCKS

If your lover says that they don't experience much erotic pleasure from being massaged, try, with great sensitivity, to discover why. Is it because they are inhibited about a particular part of their body? Have they perhaps had negative experiences of touch or massage in the past? Has erotic massage never featured in their previous relationships? Find out whether your lover would be interested in exploring erotic touch and, if so, what kind of encouragement or stimulation they need. Perhaps look at some of the ideas in this chapter to see which ones appeal to them.

Gear your approach to them as an individual. Would a slow, gentle, reassuring approach work best? If so, try the Tantric massage for her (see pages 120 – 1) or the Tantric massage for him (see pages 122–3). Alternatively, if a fun, playful approach would suit your lover better, try the undulating oil massage (see pages 76 – 7).

create an erotic toy box

You can do wonderful things with your hands, but erotic touch is made all the more fun if you introduce some props. It is easy to create a box of toys and tools from everyday objects and use them in novel ways to excite and stimulate your lover.

- Beads: a string of beads is a versatile massage tool. For example, she can wind them loosely around her lover's erect penis and rub them along the length of his shaft. Or she can kneel on all fours and he can draw the beads back and fourth across her genitals.

- Ice and water: try moving an ice cube in slow, circular movements around your lover's nipples (see right). When they are rock hard, you can warm them up again using your lips and tongue. Give your lover a hot-water massage: pour thick streams of hot water on to their belly or buttocks as they sit in the bath or give them a genital massage using a powerful jet of warm water from the showerhead.

- Feathers: the soft, fleeting touch of a feather can feel exquisite on the skin and arouse you in all sorts of subtle ways. Peacock feathers are good to use, partly because of their beautiful, exotic appearance, but also because they are long and flexible.

- Scarves: a silk scarf can produce a similar sensation to a feather. You can bring your lover's skin alive by wafting it along their body, and you can also use it to blindfold them (see below).

- Honey: drizzle honey from the collarbone, down the breasts (see far right) and on to the tummy so that it pools in the navel and creates a honey-well, before dripping down to the genitals. Remove the honey with your tongue, massaging your lover's body with licks as you go.

SIGHT DEPRIVATION

A blindfold is a fantastic tool to include in your erotic toy box. Although your lover can get a buzz from watching what you are doing during erotic massage, depriving them of sight can offer a rich experience and up the eroticism incredibly. Without sight your lover becomes much more aware of and sensitized to touch. Blindfolding your lover also sends the message that you are firmly in control – this in itself can be an amazing turn-on. And a lover who can't see will be more open to suggestion, so you can plant a whole array of wonderfully erotic images or fantasies in their mind!

penetrate the imagination

The most transcendent massage experiences happen when you engage your lover's mind as well as their body. Whispering an erotic story, fantasy or visualization during a massage can transport them – and you – into a truly blissful and private universe.

THE STORYTELLER

To make your fantasy story seem as real and erotic as possible, make it about the two of you and tell it in the first person and the present tense. Make the fantasy something that is going to appeal to you both: you need to feel comfortable telling it and your lover needs to feel enticed and drawn into a world of make-believe.

Relating a fantasy to your lover is like telling any story: it works best when it's told with confidence and filled with rich, exciting detail. Imagine you're telling an erotic story about a night-time beach seduction – give your lover details that will stimulate all five of their senses. For sight, describe the deserted beach, the moon in the sky, the trees that you're lying under. For taste and smell, describe the salty taste and smell as you lick the beads of sweat and sea from your lover's belly. For touch, tell them how the sand is grazing your skin as you kneel astride your lover. For sound, describe the waves beating on the shore.

Good stories contain an element of suspense, so don't launch into the erotic action straight away. Tantalize your lover by making them wait. Create an atmosphere of sexual tension. If, for example, your fantasy story starts in an office, talk about the way you make eye contact, or how you feel turned on, but go to great lengths to conceal it. Great material for fantasy stories includes sex outdoors, sex in public, forbidden sex, or being made to wait for sexual gratification.

When you get to the erotic action, be as specific as possible, so that your lover can really imagine what you are doing. For example, "I'm sliding my finger inside you and kissing your thighs." Use language that you feel comfortable with; you don't have to talk dirty if you don't want to – just use words that you'd use ordinarily. If you can, make the actions of your massage match what is going on in the story.

If you find it difficult to make up a fantasy story, describe a past erotic encounter that you have shared with your lover. Alternatively, ask your lover to assign you a character, such as a doctor, teacher or prostitute. It's often easier to act out a prescribed role than to be yourself. Even speaking in a different language or accent can free you from inhibition and inspire you.

THE LISTENER

As the recipient of a fantasy story, your role is to lie back and savour the pleasure of combined touch and mental imagery. Engage with the story on as many levels as you can: imagine the smells, sights, sounds and sensations that your lover is creating for you. Try to leave your everyday world far behind. Letting yourself drift completely into fantasy is a great way to stop the chatter of thoughts that normally go on in the mind. And once your mind is engaged in pure eroticism, your body will be too. Women in particular say that fantasy can lift them into much higher levels of arousal than normal and make orgasm easier and more intense.

While you're immersed in the fantasy, you can communicate how wonderful you're feeling with moans and lots of "Mmmms". If you've enjoyed a fantasy story, give your lover positive feedback and tell them which bits you found the biggest turn-on.

red-hot massage for her

Genital massage feels like an especially indulgent treat because all of her erotic hot spots receive prolonged, slow and direct attention. Your lover may experience completely different sensations from those she experiences during penetrative sex when the clitoris often receives only indirect stimulation and the vagina is more likely to receive a fast, thrusting touch than slow, static pressure. Pick a time when neither of you will be disturbed. Make yourselves comfortable and tell your lover that you are going to give her an erotic massage for as long as she wants – all she needs to do is lie back and enjoy it. As always, there should be no pressure to climax. If you have sex at any point, remember that massage oil can damage condoms.

STEP 1 **Ask your lover to lie down (or she may prefer to be slightly propped up), and then sit or kneel in between her legs. Rather than beginning the massage immediately, rest one hand on your lover's genitals and one hand between her breasts. Synchronize your breathing with your lover's and feel your connection to her through the palms of your hands.**

STEP 2 **Generously lubricate your palms with massage oil and then stroke your lover's vulva from the back to the front, palm over palm so that your hands don't break contact with her. Make your strokes long, slow and firm and let them finish on her pubic mound. For hygiene reasons, don't include her anus. Repeat these strokes for a couple of minutes.**

STEP 3 **Instead of using your palm to stroke her vulva, use your fingertip – either your index or middle finger. Let your fingertip glide along the right side of her vulva up over her clitoral hood and then back down the left side. Do this incredibly slowly and ask her if she'd like you to press harder. Keep moving your fingertip in this U shape for two or three minutes. Avoid touching her clitoris or clitoral hood – make her wait...**

STEP 4 **Gently tug sections of her pubic hair. If she likes this, do it all over her pubic mound and then work your way along her outer labia. You can also try gently tweaking and pulling her labia between your thumb and index finger. Check that she's responding positively to this.**

STEP 5 **Use the pads of your index and middle fingers to press the area on her pubic mound immediately above her clitoral hood. Slowly move your fingers in circles, getting closer and closer to her clitoris.**

Before you actually reach her clitoris, take your fingers away and replace them with just one fingertip. Use this to draw several slow clockwise circles around her clitoral hood. Then draw several slow anti-clockwise circles. Keep doing this for a few minutes – vary the speed and pressure in response to any feedback she gives you. Finally, move your finger or fingers in circles directly on her clitoris or clitoral hood.

STEP 6 **This is a stroke that incorporates clitoral and vaginal stimulation. Put one or**

more well-lubricated fingers inside your lover's vagina (ask her what feels comfortable), and gently slide them in and out, exploring and caressing her vaginal walls.

STEP 7 **Now try experimenting with some different finger movements – if you have two fingers inside your lover, try sliding them against one another. Try applying static pressure to the front wall of her vagina – the site of her G-spot (see page 67). Now, with your other hand, caress her clitoris.**

An alternative way of stimulating her vagina and her clitoris simultaneously is to insert your thumb into her vagina and rest your fingers on her clitoris – now rock your hand so that your thumb moves in and out of her vagina.

red-hot massage for him

Like women, men tend to masturbate in familiar ways that are guaranteed to bring results. There's nothing wrong with this but, over time, the same predictable touch can lose its power. This is why offering your lover a new set of massage strokes for his penis – ones that he might not use on himself – can be super-erotic. Before you begin the massage, make sure your lover is lying comfortably – semi-reclining on a bank of pillows is a good position because it is comfortable and allows him to enjoy the thrill of seeing exactly what you're doing. Tell him that you're going to massage him rather than masturbate him and that orgasm is optional. If you have sex after the massage, remember that massage oil can damage condoms.

STEP 1 **Cover your lover's penis and balls with one hand – fingers spread apart and facing his feet – and use the other hand to pour oil over the back of the first hand. The oil will drip between your fingers and nicely lubricate his genitals, making the massage easier for you and more pleasurable for him. Next, use your hands to stroke his balls and penis in long, smooth movements, one hand after the other. These strokes should gently pull his balls and penis in the direction of his head.**

STEP 2 **Grasp his penis with your hand and gently squeeze it inside your fist. Use both hands if necessary, one fist on top of the other. Do this pumping action in a rhythmic fashion, using different amounts of pressure** for variety. This stroke mimics the way that you might use your pelvic floor muscles to squeeze his penis during sex.

STEP 3 **The F-spot refers to the frenulum – the fold of skin on the underside of the penis. This is a particularly sensitive spot. Use one hand to hold the bottom of the shaft, and the thumb of the other hand to make small circular movements on the frenulum. You can also try pinching and rubbing the skin of the frenulum between your thumb and forefinger.**

STEP 4 **Interlock your fingers and wrap your hands around your lover's penis. The heels of your hands should meet on the underside of his penis. His shaft should now be tightly** enclosed in the tube made by your hands. **Make your thumbs point upward so that the pads of your thumbs rest on his frenulum. Using a firm grip, move the tube of your hands up and down on his penis. Vary the speed of your movements according to what he enjoys most.**

STEP 5 **Make sure your lover's penis is very well lubricated and grasp it in your hands – one fist on top of the other. Now twist your bottom hand in a clockwise direction and your top hand in an anti-clockwise direction. Keep your grasp firm and experiment with different speeds. If you like, you can combine the twisting motion of your hands with a simultaneous up-and-down movement. Be guided by your lover's response.**

STEP 6 **Grasp your lover's penis in one hand and draw his foreskin up and down over the head and shaft of his penis. This is the standard way that most men masturbate. The difference here is that you hold the palm of your other hand flat over the tip of his penis – on each upward stroke the head of his penis bumps gently into the flat of your palm.**

STEP 7 **This massage stroke is sometimes called the juicer. It resembles the way you might juice a lemon by twisting it back and forth on a lemon squeezer. Use one hand to draw his foreskin down his shaft. Use the fingers of your other hand to grip just below the glans. Move this hand in a twisting, up-and-down movement.**

Tease and tantalize with this erotic massage guaranteed to turn your lover on in an instant. The key is to make sure your mouth or hands don't go anywhere near your lover's genitals. By the end they will be begging for you to touch them all over and you can treat them to the genital massage techniques you've learned. They are worth waiting for...

Stand or sit very close to your lover and take their earlobe between your thumb and forefinger. Very gently caress, pull and stroke it. Now use the tip of your index finger to trace a line around the outside of the ear. Do this several times and then gently trace the curves and whorls on the inside of your lover's ear. If they find this ticklish, use a firmer touch or go back to touching the outside of the ear.

Now bring your lips close to your lover's ear and gently kiss their temple and the area around the ear. Make your kisses featherlight and barely audible. Gently suck and nibble the earlobe. To take the eroticism a notch higher, simultaneously caress your lover's nipple. Next, try probing the inside of the ear with the tip of your tongue, using the lightest of movements. Inhale and exhale so softly that your breath caresses your lover's ear. Finally, plant a row of exquisitely featherlight kisses from the ear, working your way slowly and sensually down the neck. Now your lover can have their red-hot treat (see pages 50–3).

the voluptuous vagina

Although the hands can perform all sorts of delicate manipulations there's something incomparably sexy about being massaged by the vulva and vagina. What it lacks in dexterity, it makes up for in eroticism. Many men would describe this as the ultimate massage because it is such a powerful turn-on in which the woman is completely in control.

EXTERNAL MASSAGE

Start by making sure your vulva is really lubricated. Spread some oil or lubricant on to your lover's belly and chest. Now support yourself on all fours above him so that your vulva is in contact with his belly and move your hips in slow, undulating movements so that your genitals caress his skin. Gradually move your way up his body like this. If you like you can go as far as his mouth, although the aim is for you to give him prolonged erotic pleasure, rather than for you to receive stimulation.

Next slowly work your way back down your lover's body, moving your genitals against him as you go. Take hold of his penis and rub the tip softly along the length of your vulva and then move on to the internal massage if you both wish.

INTERNAL MASSAGE

Lower yourself on to your lover's erect penis. Stay still for several seconds. Contract your vaginal muscles to their full height so that he feels tightly held, then relax them. Do this several times. Now contract your vaginal muscles, hold the contraction and move your vagina up his penis as though you were "milking" him. When you get to the tip of his penis, relax and sink back down. Do this for as long as you like and rapidly contract and relax your vaginal muscles while he is fully inside you.

THE VAGINAL WORK-OUT

This exercise will give you super-fit vaginal muscles. Insert a finger into your vagina and try to "grip" it by tensing your muscles. Put your hand on your belly as you do the work-out – your abdominal muscles should stay still. Twice a day, every day, for a month, draw up these muscles to their full height and hold them before slowly releasing them. Repeat four times. As you do this, it helps to visualize a lift ascending and descending through three floors. As your vaginal muscles get stronger, you can add more floors.

the playful penis

Next time you make love, put aside the desire to ejaculate and, instead, imagine that your penis is a massage tool with which you are going to caress both the outside and inside of your lover. By putting aside the desire to ejaculate, you can use your penis in all sorts of novel ways, rather than the fast, rhythmic thrusting that many men rely upon to come.

EXTERNAL MASSAGE

Start by making your erect penis slippery with lubricant – it needs to glide over her skin rather than drag. Support yourself on top of her and move your hips so that your penis glides smoothly over her belly, breasts and nipples. Remember to move in a way that is intended to pleasure your lover rather than heighten your own arousal.

Now, holding the shaft of your penis in one hand and supporting yourself on your other hand, rub the glans of your penis up and down the length of her vulva. Do this several times without penetrating. Next, use the tip of your penis to massage her clitoris. Use a variety of different strokes: quick, light flicks backward and forward on the clitoris; slow circles around the clitoris and then firm, static pressure.

When your lover is really turned on, let the tip of your penis slide back from her clitoris and penetrate her vagina. Make tiny thrusting movements so that only a small fraction of your penis enters her. Do this as many times as you – or she – can take it, and then penetrate her fully so that the entire length of your penis glides smoothly into her. Now stay still for several long moments. Lie closely together and synchronize your breathing with hers. Concentrate on the sense of connection between the two of you. Move on to the internal massage if you both wish.

INTERNAL MASSAGE

When you are ready, thrust in and out of your lover incredibly slowly so that you can both experience and savour the subtlety of the sensations. Every so often withdraw your penis and use it to massage her clitoris again. Experiment with moving your penis inside your lover in different ways – enter her at unusual angles so that your penis presses more against the right or the left wall of her vagina. Wriggle your hips from side to side rather than up and down. If you are becoming too aroused, move away and use your hands to stimulate her instead.

THE PENILE WORK-OUT

Just like the vagina, the penis will become stronger if it's exercised. You may also find it easier to delay ejaculation if you do this work-out regularly. There are two parts to these exercises. First, flex your penile muscles – so that your penis twitches – ten times in quick succession. Try to do this exercise three times a day. Second, imagine that your erect penis has a flag hanging from its end. The aim of the exercise is to raise the flag in stages: lift it part of the way; stop; lift it a bit more; stop; now lift it as high as it will go. When your muscles are fully contracted hold them like this, then slowly release them again in stages. Try to do this muscle-strengthening exercise at least twice a day.

mouth massage for her

Oral sex often happens between the kisses and caresses of foreplay and sexual intercourse. It's a great way of getting aroused, but rather than relegating oral sex to a few minutes of pre-sex play, it is wonderful to give – and receive – mouth massage as a sexual gift entirely in its own right.

THE WARM-UP

When your lover is lying on her back in a comfortable position, kneel between her legs and kiss her navel. Use the tip of your tongue to dip into and lick circles around her navel – this is suggestive of the oral sex that you are about to give her. Slowly kiss, nuzzle and lick in a line that extends from her navel down through her pubic hair. Pause when you get to the area above her clitoris and very gently and softly let your lips rest on this spot. Breathe out slowly and softly as if you are trying to steam up a window – she will feel this as a sensation of sensual, spreading heat.

CLITORAL STIMULATION

Use the tip of your tongue to draw circles first clockwise and then anti-clockwise around her clitoris. Aim to tantalize and build up her arousal rather than to stimulate her clitoris directly at this point. Make your tongue soft and lick the length of her vulva, pausing at her vaginal entrance to make firm swirling movements. To stimulate her clitoris directly, put your lips around the tip and suck. Then, still sucking, move the flat part or the tip of your tongue in slow, firm circles on or around her clitoris. Flick your tongue fast across her clitoris too. As her arousal builds, increase the speed of your tongue strokes and maintain a regular rhythm – take your cues from your lover's body language.

THE FOUNTAIN OF LIFE

In the tradition of Tantric sex (see page 110), the *yoni* (the name for the female genitals) is considered to be a sacred place: the birthplace of the goddess and the source of the fountain of life. As you give your lover this erotic mouth massage, imagine that you are drinking from this fountain. Concentrate on and savour the unique smells of your lover and tell her how much you love to taste her. Allow yourself to become fully immersed in the pleasure that you are giving to and receiving back from her.

mouth massage for him

One of the great things about oral sex is that the mouth is made for massage: it's warm and soft, the tongue is capable of delivering a multitude of sensations…and it comes ready-lubricated.

THE WARM-UP

Try this technique to kick-start arousal. Make an airtight seal with your lips around the base of his unerect penis. Now suck hard. This causes blood to rush into his penis. Even if it doesn't give him a full erection, it's enough to begin a mouth massage. Hold his penis at the base and lick it in long, upward strokes from the middle of the shaft to the tip of the glans. Make your tongue broad and flat as if you were licking an ice-cream.

LICKING TECHNIQUES

When he has a solid erection, hold the tip of his penis against his belly and lick the length of the underside by moving your head quickly from side to side. Then move your tongue to his frenulum and use the pointed tip of your tongue to rapidly flick this sensitive area. Now move your whole mouth over the top of his glans and as far down his shaft as you can.

THE TWO-RING TECHNIQUE

Just below your lips, encircle his penis with your thumb and forefinger. The first ring is soft because it's created by your lips; the second is harder, because it's created by your thumb and forefinger. This combination of soft and hard is highly stimulating. Move both "rings" simultaneously up and down over his glans. Alternate between slow, languorous movements and fast, slick ones. Now keep your mouth going up and down while your thumb and forefinger twists and strokes the middle of his shaft.

BALL GAMES

This erotic mouth massage can include his balls too – most men enjoy the sensation this brings. Experiment to find out what your lover likes and ask him for feedback. Use the tip of your tongue to make tiny butterfly licks and kisses on every part of his scrotum – and underneath his balls too. Or try gently sucking his balls. To put them in your mouth, use your thumb and forefinger to make a circle around the top and then gently guide them in. Some men say that it feels good if you make a humming sound as you do this.

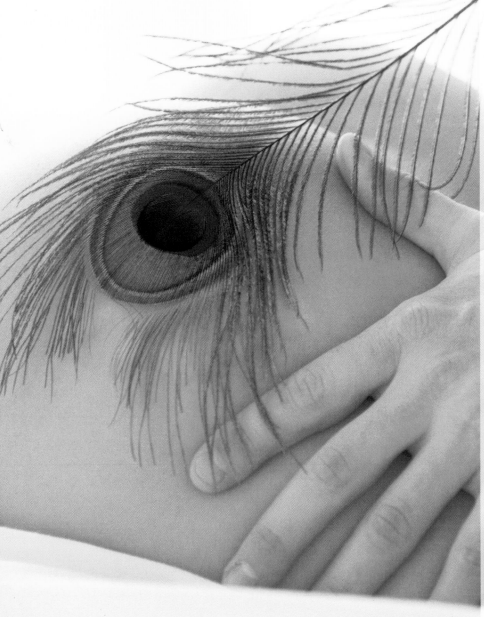

the erotic buttock

You can give your lover an array of sensations by touching their buttocks: a light "barely there" touch can bring about delicious shivers; a firm touch can cause deep-melting relaxation that penetrates to their core; stroking the perineum (the area between the anus and penis/vagina) can be a fast-track to sexual arousal.

THE WARM-UP

Start your massage with a light, tantalizing touch – lightly graze your fingernails or fingertips over the surface of your lover's buttocks. If you've got long hair, get on all fours and let the ends of your hair trail over their bum. A shaved head also creates amazing sensations. Alternatively, open your erotic toy box (see pages 46–7) and choose an object such as a paintbrush or a silk scarf to tickle and stimulate the skin.

DEEP MASSAGE

Next, rub oil into your lover's buttocks and massage the large muscles of this area using strokes such as kneading, pressing, thumb pressure and knuckling (see pages 12–15). The hands are the best tools for producing deeply relaxing and sensual sensations in the buttocks, but if you want to turn each other on, try using your mouth or your breasts. Men: pinch, suck and gently bite and nibble the flesh of your lover's buttocks. Women: rub oil into your breasts, get on all fours and slide and slither your way up your lover's legs, across his buttocks and back again.

SPANKING

Lots of men and women enjoy the sudden, stinging sensation of being spanked on the buttocks. A well-aimed spank should land on the muscles at the centre of the buttock. Keep your hand flat for a high-impact spank and slightly cupped for a more gentle spank.

PERINEAL MASSAGE

If your lover enjoys perineal massage, oil your fingers and use long strokes. For hygiene reasons, avoid touching the vagina and anus in a single stroke. Try a gentle circling stroke around the entrance to the anus, which is rich in nerve endings. If your lover enjoys it, increase the pressure on each stroke until you are massaging the inside of the opening to the anus.

g-spot massage for her

The G-spot is a unique erogenous zone. Some women have a clear idea of where it is, others aren't aware of it, and some just know that pressure on the front wall of the vagina feels good. The first secret of giving a good G-spot massage is to adopt an exploratory approach rather than expecting to press a button that yields instant results. The second is to make sure that your lover is highly aroused before you begin.

STIMULATING HER G-SPOT

Start by giving your lover a genital massage (see pages 50 – 1). When she is aroused, gently slide your index and middle finger into her vagina and use the tips to stroke the front wall of her vagina. When you feel a bump, ridge or protusion, bend your fingers into a "come here" gesture and make gentle stroking movements on this spot or area. Gradually increase the amount of pressure and ask your lover for feedback.

Some women liken the first sensations of G-spot massage to needing to urinate, but these feelings soon pass. For some women, gentle clitoral stroking or firm pressure on the lower abdomen is the crowning touch to G-spot massage. Try this, but take your cues from your lover.

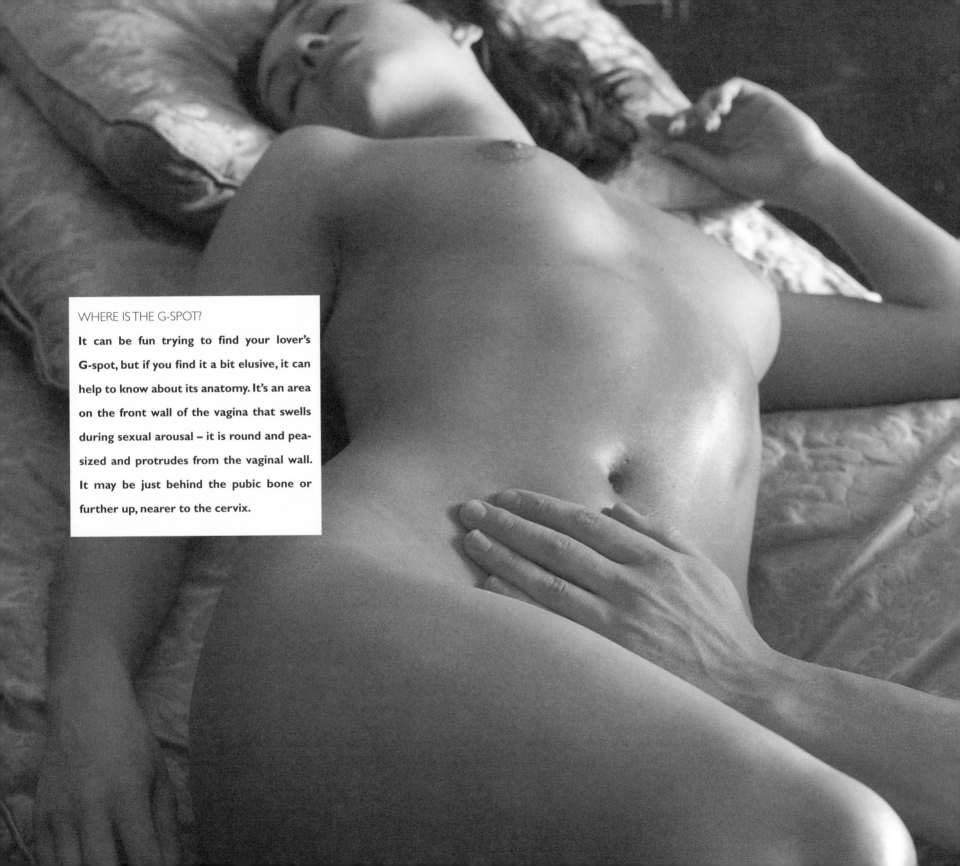

WHERE IS THE G-SPOT?

It can be fun trying to find your lover's G-spot, but if you find it a bit elusive, it can help to know about its anatomy. It's an area on the front wall of the vagina that swells during sexual arousal – it is round and pea-sized and protrudes from the vaginal wall. It may be just behind the pubic bone or further up, nearer to the cervix.

PROSTATE PLEASURE

The prostate gland is roughly walnut-sized and sits just below the bladder. When you touch this "P-spot" through the wall of the rectum, it may feel firmer or spongier than the surrounding tissue. Explore gently – when you hit the spot, your lover may have a desire to urinate, but if he relaxes and goes with the sensation it should lead to a feeling of deep and satisfying arousal.

g-spot massage for him

The male G-spot is also called the P-spot as it is found on the prostate gland. Although you can't touch the prostate gland, you can massage it "remotely" through the perineum or through the wall of the rectum.

STIMULATING HIS G-SPOT

Gently stroke, hand over hand, along the underside of your lover's erect penis until your fingers start at the tip of his penis and go all the way to his anus. Now keep your left hand on his penis and use your right hand to massage the area between his scrotum and his anus. Press quite deeply, using your fingertips or the pads of your fingers in this area. Feedback is important during this massage, so ask your lover to tell you when you hit the right spot (see left). Once you've found this spot, move your fingers in deep circles on it. This spot is sometimes called the external prostate. Aim to move the muscles beneath the skin rather than just moving the skin.

Now stimulate his G-spot through the wall of the rectum. When he is very aroused, use plenty of oil to gently insert your finger into his anus. Bend your finger in a "come here" gesture and massage the front wall of the rectum. Experiment with different strokes.

This is a unique midnight feast in which the only food you will "eat" is your lover! Lead your lover into a warm, candlelit room and tell them how you are going to feast upon their body. Your starter will be your lover's lips and mouth, your main course will be their genitals and your dessert will be their feet and toes. Many massages take place with the recipient lying down, but in this one the recipient sits up – your aim is to arouse rather than relax. Ask your lover to concentrate on receiving and tell them not to reciprocate – not even when you are kissing them.

Start by running the tip of your index finger lightly around your lover's lips. Pause every so often to push your fingertip suggestively into their mouth and moisten it with their saliva. Now bring your lips very close to your lover's, so close that they are almost touching. Stay like this for a while. Softly place your lips against your lover's and use the tip of your tongue to trace the outline of their lips. Use your lips to gently enclose your lover's lower lip. Nuzzle and suck it, but not too hard.

Move down your lover's body for the main course. Start with a genital fingertip massage, using the tip of your index finger to trace lines along every surface and contour of the vulva or penis. Now copy the course of those lines using the tip of your tongue. For dessert, sensually suck each of your lover's toes.

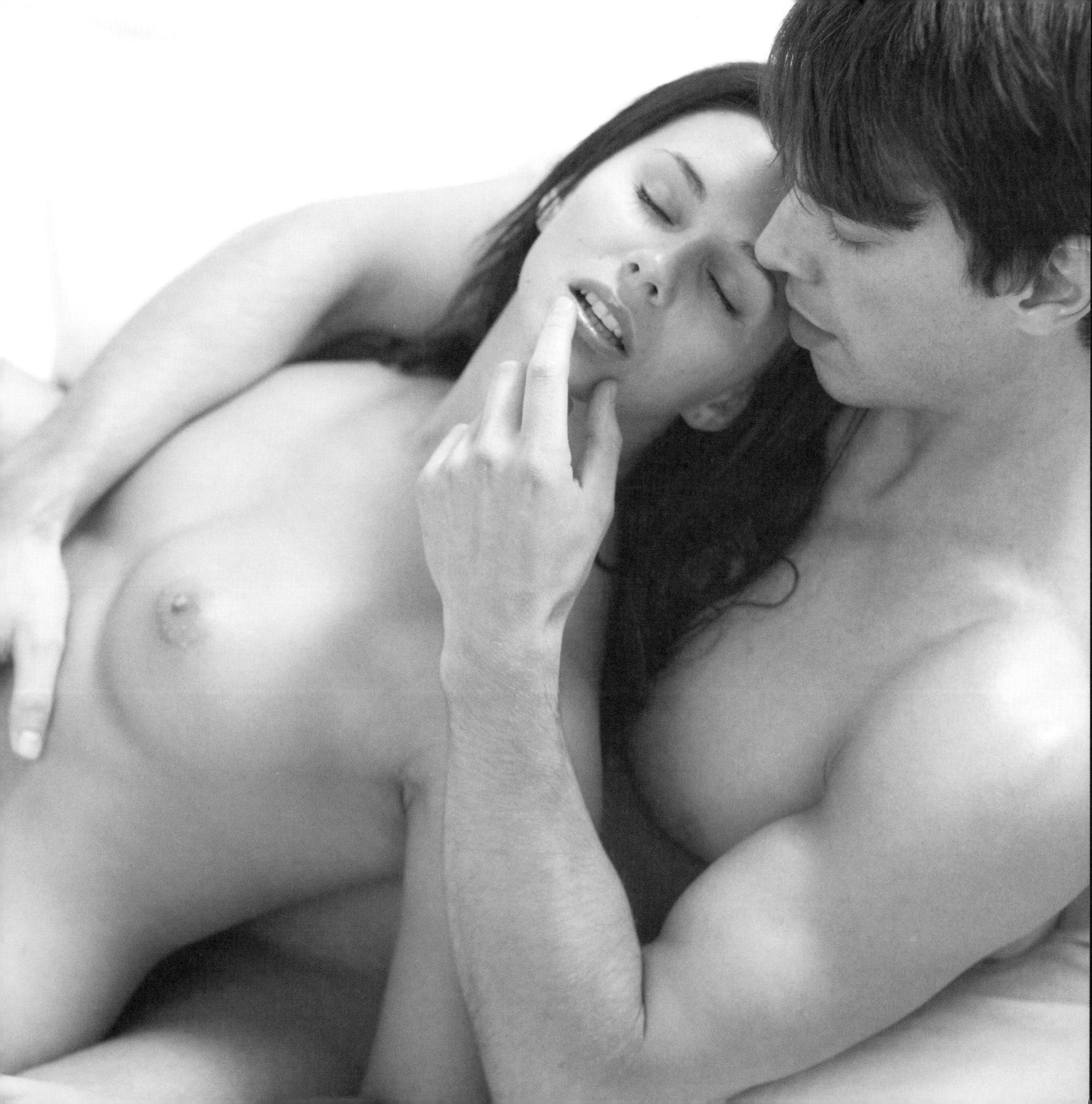

erotic breast massage

A sensual breast massage is a sure-fire way of taking many women to the peak of arousal. The secret is not to rush things – given time, some women are able to reach orgasm from nipple and breast stimulation alone.

STEP 1 **Coat your hands in oil, sit or kneel and cup your lover's breasts in your hands. Stay in this position for a few moments so that you can both savour the sensations of touching and being touched.**

STEP 2 (see left) **Slowly and gently rotate her breasts, first clockwise, then anti-clockwise. Do this for a minute or two.**

STEP 3 (see right) **Place your hands below her breasts, resting them on the rib cage, and gently caress the sides of her breasts with your thumbs. Move your palms in a diagonal** **line from the side of her lower ribs to the opposite shoulder. Keep your palms flat and your fingers pointing to the shoulder they are moving toward. Alternate stroking each breast in this way.**

STEP 4 **Let your fingertips lightly and playfully brush her nipples. Next use your thumb and fingertip to squeeze her nipples directly. Try rolling, tweaking and gentle flicking. Now pinch her nipple between the sides of your index and middle finger in a scissor position, and then flick the very tip of her nipple with your other hand.**

erotic touch games

Erotic touch is about playful and creative ways of exploring your lover's body. If you're smiling, laughing or all your senses are engaged while you're touching your lover, you know you're doing it right!

MESSAGE IN A MASSAGE

This game increases your lover's sensitivity to touch by forcing them to concentrate on the movements of your finger. Start by giving them a sensual back massage (see pages 34–5). When your lover seems relaxed and pliable, tell them that you've got a message for them. Instead of speaking the message aloud, write it in slow firm letters on their back using an oiled fingertip. Make the message as romantic or suggestive as you like – it can be one word or two, or a whole sentence. Try the same thing on your lover's belly, breasts, chest and buttocks. The aim is to discover on which spots your lover is best and worst at reading these messages.

TONGUE BATHING

One of the most sensual experiences to receive from a lover is to be licked all over – everywhere! Alex Comfort, the author of *Joy of Sex*, described this as tongue bathing. To make this into a game the lover receiving the tongue bath can hide ten small dabs of honey or maple syrup on the areas of their body they most want to be licked. The lover giving the tongue bath isn't allowed to stop until all ten dabs of honey have been discovered and thoroughly licked off! Alex Comfort recommends following this with blowing: the combination of air on wet skin can create highly erotic and mind-blowing sensations for your lover.

FINGER SUCKING

Show your lover how you like to receive oral sex by giving them mini-fellatio or cunnilingus on their finger. By watching – and feeling – what you do, your lover will quickly understand what you want.

- Men: pretend her middle finger is your penis and use your mouth, lips and tongue to lick and suck in the way you've always fantasized about.
- Women: pretend the tip of his finger is your clitoris and use your tongue to lick, suck, flick and swirl. Having gone down on each other's fingers, now try the real thing by copying all the techniques that your lover has been using on your finger.

MASSAGE BY TEETH

Tell your lover that you're going to massage them entirely with your teeth. Ask them to lie down and, if you like, blindfold them to create a sense of heightened anticipation and awareness of touch. Although the expectation of pain can cause a frisson of erotic arousal in some people, it's best to make your bites and nibbles playful rather than painful. Try these:

• The sliding bite: thoroughly lubricate your lover's skin with saliva or oil and then go to bite them. But instead of biting, let your teeth glide across the surface of the skin.

• Pinch and nibble: softly pinch your lover's flesh between your finger and thumb and then gently caress the secured flesh with your teeth. Nibble and graze rather than nip or bite.

• Love bites: create an airtight seal between your lips and your lover's skin then suck and gently graze the skin. Beware – this bite is famous for leaving a tell-tale mark. Love bites are commonly given on the neck, but feel more pleasurable on muscular areas such as the arms and buttocks.

• Fairy circles: rest your bottom teeth on your lover's toe, finger or penis and move your head in small circles. Your teeth caress rather than bite.

undulating oil massage

This is an incredibly intimate and fun massage that will up the eroticism of your lovemaking. Ensure you use lots and lots of oil so that you both get really slippery and messy.

BEFORE YOU START

Protect your bed or the floor with towels or a PVC sheet (available from sex-toy websites). Take off any jewelry and put some music on. Sit facing each other and rub each other's naked body with oil – aim to cover every surface. Get as slick and oily as possible. Abandon any concerns you have about getting messy – you can clean up later.

GET SLIPPERY

Lie on the floor and let your bodies slip and slide across each other. Don't think about what you're supposed to be doing – just move in whichever way feels natural to you. Roll over, under and across each other; twist, undulate and slide. If it helps, imagine that you are a couple of animals – seals or snakes – sliding against one another. Enjoy the sheer playfulness and sensuality of this experience.

Now take it turns to go on top and use your entire body, including your genitals, as a massage tool. When you're on top, support yourself on your hands so that you don't put too much weight on your lover. Experiment until you find the moves that feel good for you both. You could start at your lover's feet and slide incredibly slowly up their body or lie across your lover and move back and forth. Try putting your knees on either side of your lover's head and your hands on either side of their body – now slowly "dive" down the length of their body.

GET WET

After your oil massage, take a sensual shower together. Stand close together with your arms wrapped around each other and your eyes closed. Relish the sensation of water hitting and bouncing off you. Breathe in time with each other. When you feel ready, take turns to wash the oil off each other's skin. Take the opportunity to rub and caress each other with shower gel, paying particular attention to your lover's favourite erogenous zones. Then wrap each other in big towels and lie down in bed.

CHAPTER THREE

SEX TOUCH

Experience the ultimate in erotic connection by combining sex with massage. This chapter introduces you to 13 sex positions – some from Eastern erotic classics such as the *Kama Sutra* and the *Ananga Ranga* – and tells you how to massage yourself and your lover while you're in them. By using massage during lovemaking, you can slow sex down and turn it into a longer, more tactile whole-body experience that can take you to new heights of sexual pleasure.

upper hands

This is the classic woman-on-top position. The man lies on his back and the woman sits astride him in a face-to-face position. She can put her knees on the floor or, for deeper penetration, she can put her feet flat on the floor and have her knees close to her chest. If she has strong thigh muscles, she can squat rather than sit, and then raise herself up and down on his penis.

Many women say that Upper Hands is a favourite position in which to reach orgasm because they are free to move in whatever way they want at the speed that they want. On an anatomical level, Upper Hands means that the clitoris is in close contact with the man's pubic bone – lots of friction between the clitoris and the pubic bone can be, quite literally, orgasmic.

Upper Hands is a versatile position. You can make it warm and loving by gazing into each other's eyes and kissing. Or she can make it wild and raunchy by throwing her head back, pushing her breasts out and arching her spine. If she has a supple spine, she can place her hands by his feet and curve her spine back – almost like doing a backbend – and then gently gyrate her hips.

MASSAGING YOURSELF

For her: **massage your clitoris with a vibrator. Try wedging it between your clitoris and his pubic bone or hold it in your hand and move it back and forth on your clitoris. He will feel the vibrations in the base of his penis.**

For him: **using a lubricated finger, draw circles around your nipples. Start with big circles and gradually make them smaller until your finger is directly on your nipple. Try tweaking and pinching your nipples as you get close to orgasm.**

MASSAGING YOUR LOVER

For her: **support yourself on one hand and use the other hand to reach around and caress his perineum and anus. Experiment with gentle and deep pressure. Use plenty of warmed-up lubricant to create soft and slippery sensations.**

For him: **Upper Hands is a great position for giving a clitoral massage – use your fingers or thumb in circular movements or keep your hand still against your lover's clitoris, then let her move backward and forward at her own pace.**

rear straddle

An erotic alternative to the more common face-to-face, woman-on-top position, the Rear Straddle is loved by both men and women for its sheer sexiness. It's easy to get into: he lies on his back and she simply sits astride him with her back to him. If her thigh muscles are strong enough, she can try squatting instead of sitting.

The woman is very much in control in this position – both in terms of depth of penetration and movement. She can move as much or as little as she wants. She can grind, thrust, circle her hips or move up and down on his penis. Alternatively, she can sit still and just contract her vaginal muscles around his penis. He, meanwhile, is forced into the eroticism of submission because, apart from bending his knees, he can't move very much. You both have the exhilaration of anonymity because you can't see each other's faces, making this a great position for abandoning yourself to a favourite erotic fantasy.

While he is helpless, there are several ways in which the woman can vary the straddle: she can lie back while he embraces her; she can bend forward between his legs; she can put her feet between his legs; or, if she's feeling athletic, she can swivel round to face her lover.

MASSAGING YOURSELF

For her: **use your hands to massage your breasts and tweak your nipples in this position. Alternatively, reach down and move your fingers in circles around your clitoris. When you feel close to orgasm, put your other palm on your lower abdomen and apply firm, static pressure.**

For him: **rake your fingertips lightly over your lips, neck, chest and abdomen.**

MASSAGING YOUR LOVER

For her: **reach down and lightly stroke his testicles. Alternate this with deep, firm, static pressure on a spot in the perineum halfway between his scrotum and anus – this is his G-spot (see page 68).**

For him: **press your fingers into the top of her back and slide them down either side of her spine in a single stroke. Do this when she is near climax for an electrifying effect.**

skin-to-skin

This is a wonderful position for slow, soulful, intimate sex in which the fronts of your bodies are pressed closely together. You can gaze into each other's eyes, whisper into each other's ear and kiss passionately. The easiest way to get into this position is for the man to lie on his back and the woman to sit astride him.

Once she's guided his penis into herself she can get into a lying position. Although you don't have much freedom to move in this position, certain techniques can be highly stimulating. She can try resting her feet on top of his and push herself off against them; meanwhile he can help by guiding her body up and down. Alternatively, she can rest her feet on the floor, he can hold her, and then she wiggles her hips from side to side as though she is trying to shake his penis inside her. He can move his hips too.

The higher up the woman's pelvis is on the man's body, the more clitoral stimulation she receives (this combined with mutual wiggling is often recommended by sex therapists to help women achieve an orgasm during intercourse). The Skin-to-skin position can be even more arousing if you each oil the front of your body so that she can slide up and down his body effortlessly.

MASSAGING YOURSELF

For her: **before you make love, cover the front of your body with oil. Peel the top half of your body away from your lover during sex and rub your breasts and nipples in circular movements as if you were trying to spread the oil.**

For him: **ask your lover to lie still while you walk your index and middle fingers slowly and firmly up and down on the sides of your buttocks and thighs.**

MASSAGING YOUR LOVER

For her: **take one of his fingers and put it gently between your lips. Slowly take it deeper into your mouth and lick, suck and caress it with your tongue. Gaze into his eyes as you do this.**

For him: **use your fists, fingers and thumbs to apply deep, static pressure to the muscles of her buttocks, and then try gently slapping her buttocks too.**

tightly pressed

The woman feels very deeply penetrated in this position because her knees are so tightly pressed to her chest. Called the Position of Indrani in the *Kama Sutra,* this technique is recommended for men with a small penis because it gives the woman such a feeling of fullness. Of course, men with a large penis can make love in this position too, but they may not be able to thrust so freely. The greater the woman's arousal, the better able she is to accommodate the man in the Tightly Pressed position – this is because, during the peak of arousal, the upper part of the vagina expands and the uterus lifts up.

There's plenty of scope for variety for both partners. The woman can cross her feet behind his back, lower her legs into a classic missionary position or, if she's supple, she can rest one or both of her ankles on his shoulders or place the soles of her feet against his chest. He can kneel upright or lean over her body to kiss her.

This is a great way to enjoy slow and sensual lovemaking as he gently thrusts in and out of her. The man will enjoy the dominance of being in this semi-upright and visually stimulating position, which gives him lots of opportunities for erotic touch and intimate eye contact.

MASSAGING YOURSELF

For her: **use your fingers to caress your feet and pinch and squeeze your toes – imagine drawing erotic energy down from your genitals to your toes as you do so.**

For him: **if you kneel up in this position, you can tweak your nipples. You can also use one hand to squeeze the base of your penis as you thrust. This is useful if your erection is flagging because it helps to keep blood inside the penis.**

MASSAGING YOUR LOVER

For her: **ask your lover to stay still inside you, then clasp his head in your hands. Apply firm static pressure on either side of his head and stay like this to enjoy the moment fully. Gaze deeply into his eyes, and roughly run your fingers through his hair.**

For him: **stay perfectly still inside her and use one fingertip to gently caress your lover's face, neck and shoulders.**

close and entwined

You can't get much closer to your lover than this – you're quite literally wrapped up in each other. The easiest way to get into this position is to start in the missionary position or a woman-on-top position and then roll a little way on to your sides so his weight is not fully upon her. Your scope for movement is quite limited in this position but it's a great one for enjoying a long passionate kiss with your lover, and for holding each other tight and relishing the intimacy of so much skin-to-skin contact.

You can move by rocking against each other or one of you can thrust gently against the other. Or she can contract and relax her vaginal muscles around his penis (practise the vaginal work-out on page 57 to get super-fit muscles). According to the author of the 15th-century erotic classic, the *Ananga Ranga*, with practice a woman can use her muscles to squeeze the penis in the same way that "the hand of the Gopala-girl milks the cow".

A variation of this position is for the woman to have one of her legs in between her lover's legs instead of around the outside of his body. Some women find this more stimulating because there is increased pressure and friction on the clitoris.

MASSAGING YOURSELF

For her: **place your palm lightly on your thigh and slide it down your leg in a long, slow movement. Imagine that you are pushing erotic energy down toward your foot. Feel your leg and foot pulsating and tingling with pleasure.**

For him: **put your middle fingertip in the cleft at the top of your buttocks and gently massage this spot.**

MASSAGING YOUR LOVER

For her: **press your fingers into the muscles on either side of the top of his spine and then slowly slide them down the length of his back.**

For him: **put your hands under her buttocks and knead them. Grasp them firmly as you guide her toward and away from you. The buttocks can take lots of pressure, but if in doubt, ask her for feedback.**

wide open

She lies on her back with a cushion or pillow placed beneath her bottom and he kneels in between her legs and enters her. He can support himself by holding on to her waist, her legs or her hands. The cushions raise her pelvis, which makes her vagina more accessible and facilitates deeper penetration. In the 15th-century erotic classic, the *Ananga Ranga*, this technique is known as "raising the seat of pleasure". Experiment with using different amounts of numbers or pillows until you get the angle of penetration that feels good for both of you.

This is an "equal" position in that the man and woman can take it in turns to lead. He can thrust and move from side to side, while she can raise her pelvis and move her hips in circular or undulating movements. For variety she can let her knees flop out to the sides or raise her legs and place her feet on his chest; he can lean over her body and take his weight on his hands. Because of the angle of this position and the fact that she can control the thrusting, there is a good chance of her having an orgasm through clitoral stimulation.

If you want more intimacy, he can pull her up by her arms and you can wrap your arms around each other for a mid-sex cuddle.

MASSAGING YOURSELF

For her: **rest your palms on your nipples so that they are barely touching them, then move them in circles so they just graze the tips of your nipples. Increase the pressure as you become more aroused.**

For him: **coat your hands in oil and rub them against your nipples, chest and belly. (If you are using a condom, don't let it come into contact with the oil.)**

MASSAGING YOUR LOVER

For her: **sensually caress his fingers one by one and slide your palms up and down his hands and forearms at the same speed and rhythm as his thrusts.**

For him: **massage her pubic mound by moving the heel of your hand in circles just at the place where her labia start. You can also tweak her pubic hair and use the pad of your thumb to massage her clitoris.**

yawning position

This position is from the Eastern erotic classic, the *Kama Sutra*. The woman lies on her back and raises her legs so that they are at right angles to her body. The man guides his penis inside her in a kneeling position and she rests her legs along the front of his body (ideal for some toe kissing and nibbling). This position offers a tantalizing combination of intimacy and distance – you can gaze into each other's eyes but you can't quite get close enough to kiss.

You might find the Yawning Position more comfortable and easier if she places one or two cushions or pillows under her bottom. This raises and tilts her pelvis, making her vagina more accessible. Experiment until you discover the angle that feels good.

If you both enjoy deep penetration, she can bring her knees down to touch her shoulders – she needs to have supple legs and quite flexible hips to do this. Her feet can rest over his shoulders or flat on his chest. Because the penis goes so deeply into the vagina in the Yawning Position, the man should thrust gently at first. Alternatively, the woman can guide her lover's movements by resting her hands on his waist and pushing and pulling him.

MASSAGING YOURSELF

For her: **use a long feather, such as a peacock feather, to stroke your legs from foot to thigh. See if you can manage to give yourself goosebumps.**

For him: **put your hands on your buttocks and knead and pinch them. Lots of men clench their buttocks tightly when having sex in this position – keeping them relaxed can help to enhance pleasure.**

MASSAGING YOUR LOVER

For her: **walk your index and middle fingers up the large muscles of his thighs and buttocks. When you get to his waist, walk them back again. The thigh and buttock muscles can take lots of pressure, so press quite hard.**

For him: **reach down and hold your penis at the base of the shaft. Withdraw your penis and use it as a massage tool, flicking the tip back and forth across her clitoris. Alternate this with a minute of thrusting inside her every so often.**

drawing the bow

If you enjoy having sex with him positioned behind, this is a great variation on doggie-style sex or spooning. You both lie on your side – him behind her – and she sandwiches his body between her legs. She leans forward to take hold of his calves or feet. He enters her and rests his hands on her shoulders. Alternatively, you can start off in the Rear Straddle (see pages 82–3) and gently roll over on to your sides.

This is a great position for sex that's slow, lazy and leisurely. Because it's a restful rear-entry position that doesn't involve any pressure or weight-bearing, it's also good for women during late pregnancy. The man is limited in how freely he can thrust, but, instead of making vigorous movements, you can lie still together savouring the sensation of being joined, and breathing deeply in time with each other.

She can stimulate herself by touching her clitoris and stimulate him by contracting her vaginal muscles around his penis. If you want to ramp up the pace at any point, you can both roll over on to your fronts and move into a doggie-style sex position. Because there is distance between your upper bodies this isn't a very intimate position, but you can end by moving into a more loving spooning position.

MASSAGING YOURSELF

For her: **place the palm of your hand on your belly and caress your navel. Imagine drawing erotic energy from your genitals so that the whole area feels hot and tingling.**

For him: **rest your middle finger on the bridge of your nose. Apply firm pressure, close your eyes and "look" toward the point that you are pressing. Leave thoughts behind and be present solely in your body.**

MASSAGING YOUR LOVER

For her: **hold his feet in your hands and press deeply into the soles of his feet with your fingers. Slowly slide your fingers in and out of the spaces between his toes.**

For him: **press your thumbs into the muscles at the base of her neck and along the back of her shoulders. Move your thumbs in slow, firm circles so that the muscle tissue moves rather than just the skin.**

knees and elbows

While she supports herself on her knees and elbows, he penetrates her from behind. Lots of couples love the raw animalism of this position and the freedom of movement it offers. He can also penetrate her quite deeply. To achieve maximum penetration, she should push up her bottom as high as possible.

He can ramp up the sexual tension in this position by varying the rhythm and depth of his thrusts. For example, he could mix shallow strokes that just penetrate her vaginal entrance with deep strokes that stimulate her G-spot. Or he could alternate thrusting with wiggling his hips from side to side.

There are several variations of the Knees and Elbows position. She can raise her body so that it is parallel to his; or he can penetrate her in a deep squatting position instead of a kneeling position. If you do the position on the floor (instead of leaning on a bed), she can sink her chest to the ground and he can penetrate her more deeply. If she is strong enough to support her body weight on her arms, he can lift her legs off the ground and hold them on either side of his waist – this position is called "the wheelbarrow".

MASSAGING YOURSELF

For her: **reach down and place your index and middle finger on either side of your clitoris – now squeeze them together and apart in a scissor-like motion. Alternatively, hold them clamped together. This creates different sensations from the usual way that you might stroke your clitoris – close your eyes and enjoy the feelings.**

For him: **reach one hand behind you to gently caress your perineum as you move in and out of your lover.**

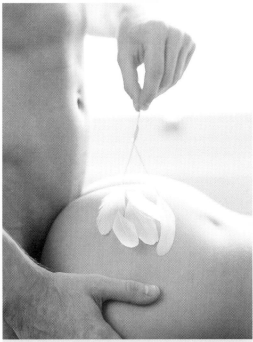

MASSAGING YOUR LOVER

For her: **try resting your feet on top of your lover's calves and caressing him with your toes.**

For him: **make the most of having free access to her buttocks – use the tips of your fingers, a feather (or any other improvized massage toy) to tickle her; if she prefers a firmer touch, press your knuckles into her buttocks and twist firmly.**

lap moves

This is a great position when you're in the mood for passionate spur-of-the-moment sex, and it is a refreshing change from making love in the bedroom. He sits on a chair and she simply straddles him. While you can take your clothes off, it isn't essential if you want a real "quickie". He simply drops his trousers and if she's wearing a dress or skirt, she just hitches it up and climbs on top.

She's in control of most of the movement, so it's a great position for her to orgasm. She can slide up and down on his penis by standing and lowering herself. If she wants more control, she can put her feet on the seat of the chair and steady herself by clasping her hands behind her lover's neck – from this squatting position she can move up and down. Alternatively, you can both rub oil or lubricant into your thighs so that you slip and slide around on each other (don't use oil if you're using a condom, though).

Depending on his strength and her weight, he can move from a sitting to a standing position with her legs clasped around his waist. If there's a wall nearby, he can stand with his back to it and she can push against it with her feet so that she moves back and forth on his penis.

MASSAGING YOURSELF

For her: **rest your fingertip on your lips. Slowly suck your finger into your mouth and gently caress it using your tongue and teeth. This is sensual for you but it will also give him a thrill!**

For him: **your movement will be reasonably limited in this position, but if she's holding on to the chair you can let go of her to enjoy some erotic self-touch. Caress your chest, tweak your nipples and run your hands firmly up and down your thighs in time with her movements.**

MASSAGING YOUR LOVER

For her: **cover your upper body with oil or lubricant. Move slowly up and down on him and twist from side to side, letting your breasts slide over his lips.**

For him: **massage her with your mouth. Flick the point of your tongue across her nipples; lick a line between her breasts and blow along the length of it; gently bite and suck her arms; use your lips to nuzzle the undersides of her breasts where they join her body; plant a row of kisses along her collarbone and then end with a proper kiss.**

spoons position

The Spoons Position is one that lots of lovers both sleep and make love in. It's comfortable, intimate and neither partner dominates. It facilitates unhurried, restful sex but with the intense sensations that deep penetration from behind can bring. After sex, you can stay in the Spoons Position and savour the relaxed closeness of your bodies (although if he is wearing a condom, he should withdraw from her before he loses his erection). It is an ideal position during the later stages of pregnancy when her belly becomes too big for face-to-face sex.

There are several variations of the Spoons Position that you can try. She can experiment by having one leg straight and one leg bent. For deeper penetration she can raise her knees so that they are closer to her body – the higher she raises them, the deeper he can penetrate. To give her better access to her clitoris, she can open her legs and hook her top leg over her lover. He can experiment with the angle at which he enters her – if he gets the right angle, his penis can hit her G-spot and produce intense erotic sensations. If you want to move into another position, he can roll on to his back, taking her with him – now she can sit up in the Rear Straddle position (see pages 82–3).

MASSAGING YOURSELF

For her: **reach down and put your fingers between your legs so that they are near or touching your clitoris. If you cannot move your hand because your thighs are closed, keep your hand still and rock your hips backward and forward to create friction this way instead.**

For him: **squeeze your penis at the base as you move in and out of your lover. This adds pressure and maintains your erection.**

MASSAGING YOUR LOVER

For her: **reach behind his head and use your nails and fingertips to tickle and caress the back of his neck.**

For him: **when your lover is extremely aroused, press your fingers firmly into the muscles of her thigh (as low down her leg as you can reach), then, keeping the pressure constant, slide your fingers tantalizingly slowly up the length of her thigh.**

face-to-face

This is one of the best positions for feeling intimately connected and at one with each other. Being seated face-to-face is often the recommended position during Tantric sex because you can stay in it for a long time near the peak of arousal. It is stimulating enough to keep you aroused, but not so stimulating that orgasm is impossible to avoid. What is most important is that in this position you are face to face with your lover, which means that you can gaze into each other's eyes, kiss tenderly and enjoy some really sensual lovemaking.

To get into the Face-to-face position, he sits cross-legged on the floor or bed and she sits astride him with her legs wrapped around his body and her feet behind his back. He can place a cushion or a pillow on his lap for her to sit on if this is more comfortable.

You can move easily from this position into a man-on-top or a woman-on-top position. You can also both fall gently on to your sides. Or, if you want to try something different, hold each other's hands and slowly lower yourselves backward so that you are lying down with your heads at opposite ends of the bed. Straighten your legs. Keep holding hands and pull and push against each other.

MASSAGING YOURSELF

For her: **lean back on one hand to support yourself and use your other hand to press and rub the area just in front of your clitoris. If he leans back slightly, he will be able to enjoy watching the proceedings.**

For him: **use the backs of your hands to brush the skin of your legs.**

MASSAGING YOUR LOVER

For her: **use your thumb and forefinger to pinch, stroke and tweak your lover's earlobe. At the same time, kiss him softly on the lips.**

For him: **use your hands to massage her back in long, smooth strokes that go from her shoulders all the way down to her buttocks and back up again. Graze with your fingernails for a more erotic touch.**

up close and personal

This is a great position for spontaneous sex, especially if you're in an enclosed space – such as a shower – or there's no bed or other convenient surface on which to lie down. She simply puts her arms around his neck and wraps one leg around his waist. He will probably need to bend his knees a little in order to penetrate her. This can be a precarious position, so look for a nearby wall – either of you can lean against it for balance and stability.

How well this position works depends on how tall you are in relation to each other (it doesn't work very well if he is much taller than her). If he can't penetrate her – or he can only achieve shallow penetration – she can help by wearing high heels, standing on tiptoe, raising her leg high on his body, or standing on a raised surface such as a step. Alternatively, he can bend into a deep squat, or pick her up so that both her legs are around his waist. There isn't a lot of freedom of movement in this position, but the slow, careful movements of his penis can make up for this in eroticism. If you want a position in which he can thrust more freely, she can turn around and he can penetrate her from behind while both of you are standing.

MASSAGING YOURSELF

Since Up Close and Personal is often used for impromptu sex, there may not be much time for foreplay. So if you know you're in the mood for a quickie, you might want to indulge in some self-massage beforehand.

For her: **use your fingers to caress your G-spot, vagina and clitoris before you have sex – the more aroused you are, the easier it will be for your lover to penetrate you in a standing position.**

For him: **firmly stroke the length of your penis before sex so that you are as hard as possible; as you penetrate her, grip your penis firmly around the base of the shaft to maintain the firmness of your erection.**

MASSAGING YOUR LOVER

For her: **use your lips and tongue to nuzzle, lick and kiss the sensitive spots along the sides of your lover's neck and along the line of his jaw.**

For him: **press your fingers firmly into the centre of her buttock and then move them in a slow, firm line along the underside of her raised thigh and back again. Use oil to make the movement smooth.**

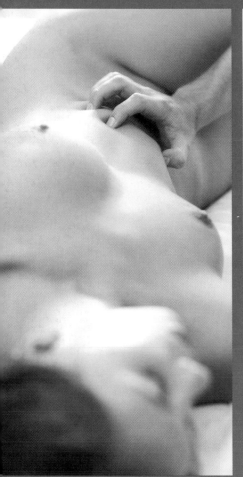

Get your lover in the mood for trying some new positions with this highly erotic touch technique. It is a particularly good way of reviving them after a long, hard day at work, and will put them in the mood for some sexual adventure. Get into bed together and ask your lover to roll on to their belly. Make your hands into claw shapes and, keeping your fingers strong, stroke their calves, thighs and buttocks. Ask your lover whether they prefer a light or firm touch – always be guided by them.

Move on to "clawing" your lover's back, shoulders and arms. When you get to their neck and head, use just your thumb and index and middle fingers. Now that your lover is relaxed and their sensitivity heightened, ask them to roll over on to their back. Use your fingers to lightly claw the area around their belly – keep your strokes moving downward, getting tantalizingly closer to the genitals with each stroke. Ask your lover to open their legs and use just the index and middle finger to "claw" and stroke down from the navel. When the man is the masseur, he should stroke over her pubic triangle and along the length of her vulva. When the woman is the masseur, she can move her fingertips along the length of his shaft and down across his balls and perineum. After enjoying this erotic touch, you will hopefully both feel energized, so take your pick of one – or more! – of the positions from this chapter.

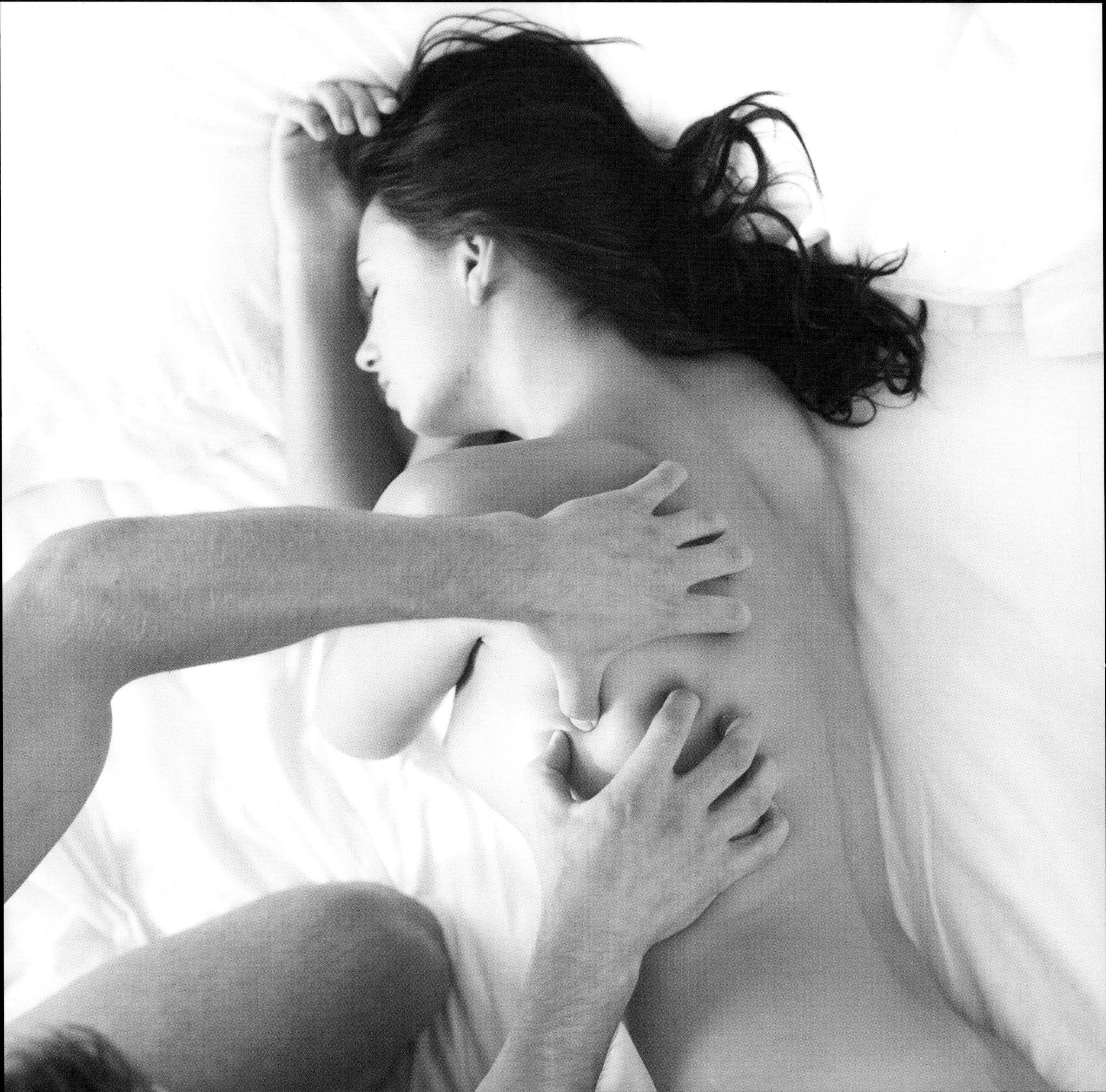

CHAPTER FOUR

TANTRIC TOUCH

Tantric touch takes sensual massage to the next level.

If you practise Tantric exercises regularly, you'll learn

that as well as giving and receiving erotic pleasure, you

can also give and receive erotic energy. As you hold

your hands above your lover's skin you will begin to

feel the pulse and tingle of energy flowing through your

fingertips. You can use this energy to heal your

lover, free them of tension and even take them to a

new plane of sensual awareness.

discover tantric touch

The practices in this chapter are intended to give you a taste of Tantra through Tantric touch techniques. Tantra means different things to different people. A popular view is that it's a set of esoteric and mysterious sexual practices and rituals. Yet for those who have experienced Tantra, it can represent a very practical way to improve the sensual and sexual bond between lovers.

THE POWER OF TANTRIC TOUCH

You can benefit in many ways from using Tantric touch techniques. You can start to heal the body of tension that it may have been storing for many years, you and your lover can become lost in the playfulness of the moment and you can stimulate the "energy body" and encourage the flow of energy through the chakras (see below).

MOVING ENERGY THROUGH TOUCH

In Tantric teaching, as well as having a physical body, we also have an energetic or a "subtle" body that consists of channels and chakras. The word "chakra" means "wheel" and refers to a spinning circle of light where energy is concentrated. There are seven chakras in the body and they are situated in line with the spinal cord. Each one represents a different level or plane of awareness. The first chakra is on the perineum and the seventh chakra is at the crown of the head. The ones in between are situated at the lower abdomen, the solar plexus, the heart, the throat and the brow. Using massage you can move energy up through the chakras (see pages 118–9) – this can have a wonderful effect on your lover, leaving them feeling refreshed and relaxed.

HARNESSING SEXUAL ENERGY

One of the core aims of Tantra is to harness sexual energy and, rather than dissipate it "externally" through orgasm, redirect it up through the chakras. When this energy reaches the chakras of the heart and head, awareness expands and people report blissful or ecstatic experiences.

As the Tantric teacher Margot Anand says: "Most lovemaking is very dynamic. You move vigorously, and you breathe hard, building up sexual passion until you explode the energy outward in a final release. In contrast, the orgasm of the brain resembles the smooth, endless gliding of a kite in the wind. You enter effortlessly into a sense of floating, as if the boundaries of your body were expanding." Many people who practise Tantric exercises also describe a sensation of communion with their lover at peak moments; a feeling that they are merging into one another. By using Tantric touch techniques such as fingertip stroking (see pages 124 – 5) you can build erotic bliss slowly and gradually so that sex becomes a long and extremely pleasurable sensual voyage.

TANTRA IN PRACTICE

The practices involved in Tantric sex include visualization, eye contact, massage, breathing exercises and muscular contractions. These are practised both during intercourse and separately. Their combined effect is to turn touching into a meditative activity in which you are fully focused only on the present moment.

In contrast to popular belief, Tantric practices aren't a fast-track to mind-blowing sex, so you and your lover shouldn't expect too much too soon – the blissful, meditative experiences offered by Tantra are subtle and can take time to happen.

dissolving body armour

We could all have a much greater lovemaking experience if we managed to rid ourselves of everyday stresses and worries. In addition – to experience the full height of eroticism during sex – Tantric teachers say that we must first get rid of the tension that has accumulated in our bodies over months and years – even over a lifetime.

Many of us carry around muscle tension that results from the negative emotional experiences we undergo in life. When something difficult or traumatic happens we tense up and "store" the experience in our bodies. The consequence of this is that instead of being open, vibrant and sensitive, over time the body starts to become closed, and insensitive to touch. Energy, rather than flowing freely around the body, becomes blocked and limits our sexual experiences and pleasure.

WHAT IS ARMOURING?

The process of physically shutting down in response to negative experiences is known as body armouring – a concept developed by the Austrian/American psychiatrist and psychoanalyst Wilhelm Reich (1897–1957). Although body armouring is the body's way of protecting itself from pain and trauma, it also results in a diminished ability to experience physical pleasure and sensuality.

GENITAL ARMOURING

Tantric teachers say that the genitals are as susceptible to armouring as any other part of the body. Genital armouring can be the result of unpleasant or traumatic sexual experiences. In women it can also be due to traumatic experiences of surgery such as abortion or hysterectomy.

A simple and common cause of genital armouring in both sexes is the negative messages we may receive about our genitals during childhood. For example, being told off for touching our genitals or being taught that our genitals are shameful in some way.

Genital armouring can manifest itself in the following ways:

- Little sensitivity or sensation during sex.
- Little sensitivity or sensation during masturbation.
- Not being able to reach orgasm or not experiencing very powerful or satisfying orgasms.
- Needing lots of hard and fast genital stimulation.

• The muscles around the anus, vagina and penis may be chronically tense – this makes it hard to "let go" and embrace erotic and sensual pleasure fully.

HEALING MASSAGE

Tantric massage is designed to overcome genital armouring by slowly and systematically massaging away tension. The spirit in which the massage is given is more important than the actual massage techniques that are used. If you are giving a healing Tantric massage, your approach needs to be gentle, loving, supportive and compassionate.

If you are receiving Tantric massage, it helps to acknowledge the fact that you may experience difficult emotional and physical feelings. Some people report having flashbacks to particular sexual events as a specific part of the genitals is massaged.

What makes Tantric massage different from any other genital massage is the intention behind it (to heal rather than to arouse) and also the preparation you do beforehand. Rituals such as creating – and being in – a sacred space (see page 114) and the sensual awakening exercise (see pages 116 – 17) help to put you in a mindful state that makes you receptive to healing.

Lovers often report that Tantric massage makes them more intimate with one another because it involves a high level of vulnerability and trust. Also, as massage dissolves tension and the genitals begin to heal, sensitivity and sensation return, making sex a more sensual and erotic experience for both partners.

BEING IN THE MOMENT

Feeling absorbed in touch, sensation and eroticism is a core part of Tantric sex in general. The emphasis is on being in the moment and immersing yourself in physical sensation rather than thinking about what you should be doing.

Tantric teachers often advocate a sense of fun and playfulness in Tantric exercises. By returning to a childlike state of wonder and joy, we are able to connect more deeply with ourselves and with our lovers. To experience the playfulness of physical touch try the undulating oil massage (see pages 76 – 7).

the sex sanctuary

There's a strong emphasis on ritual in Tantric sex. Rituals help to focus the mind and draw a line between everyday life and the ceremonial. Creating an environment in which you and your lover can enjoy each other's body is a way of saying: "We care about this, we're going to celebrate each other and we're not going to rush." Even if you can't make a room into a permanent sanctuary, it's worth transforming your bedroom or living room just for a day or an evening.

CREATING A SANCTUARY

How would you describe the room in which you massage and make love with your partner? Does it feel like a sanctuary in which you can abandon yourself to pleasure? Or are you distracted by reminders of everyday life – things such as a television, work papers or a pile of laundry?

The first part of creating a sanctuary involves removing any items that have the potential to distract you during lovemaking. Remove anything that can make a noise: radios, clocks, telephones, computers or televisions. Clean the room and remove any clutter – your aim is to create the most bare, clean and functional space possible.

A SENSUAL DELIGHT

Create an environment that is not just visually appealing, but which also feels, smells and sounds seductive. Choose silky fabrics in rich colours such as red, gold or orange, favourite pictures or ornaments, and natural objects such as shells, stones, petals or flowers. Choose sheets, throws, cushions and pillows that feel good on your skin; burn incense or essential oil; put on some unobtrusive music (chanting at a low volume can create a great ambience) or hang some wind chimes near an open window.

THE FLICKER OF CANDLELIGHT

Changing the lighting in a room is a fast and effective way to change its mood and ambience. Using several lamps rather than a single overhead light creates a soft, inviting feel, but the most magical and seductive form of lighting is the flicker of candlelight. Candles have always played an important role in sacred rituals, and candlelight is often associated with romance, mystery and peace. Also, if you or your lover feel exposed or self-conscious when you are naked, the softness of candlelight can help you to relax and feel more confident.

sensual awakening through tantra

To wake up the body truly and revitalize your lover's senses, try these sensual awakening techniques. It's a wonderful and intimate ritual to enjoy with your lover before giving them a Tantric massage. At the end your lover will feel more fully alive, sensitized and in the moment.

You are going to give your lover a series of sensual treats, so you need to devote some thought to what these will be in advance – there are plenty of ideas below. For the first four stages of the exercise, your lover should be blindfolded – depriving them of sight will force them to concentrate on their other senses.

GETTING PREPARED

Start by sitting with your lover in your sex sanctuary. Take all or most of your clothes off, but make sure you're both warm enough. Spend a few minutes relaxing together in whatever way you like: cuddling, chatting, kissing, sitting close to one another with your eyes closed or meditating. When you're both ready, tell your lover that you're going to put a blindfold on them and that all they need to do is to sit back and relish the treats that you're about to deliver.

STAGE 1

Using essential oils is a wonderful way to stimulate your lover's sense of smell. Pick a selection of three or four oils: eucalyptus, peppermint, ylang ylang, rosemary, jasmine, geranium and sandalwood are all good choices. If you know your lover prefers particular scents, choose those. Tell your lover that you are going to give them some oils to smell. Slowly pass each bottle under their nose several times. Ask them to inhale deeply as you do so and to take ten breaths in between each different smell. This will allow them to fully experience each smell, one at a time. End this stage of the sensual awakening by spraying one of the essential oils into the air so that a fine mist of fragrant water falls on to your lover's face and hair.

STAGE 2

Ask your lover to turn their attention to their sense of hearing. First, they should concentrate on the sounds that are furthest away – those that are outside the room or the building – and after this bring their awareness to the sounds that are closest to them. Then turn your attention to your breathing. Breathe deeply in and out together and ask your lover to concentrate on the sound of your combined breath.

Now give your lover some magical sounds to stimulate them – think of them as food for the ears. Play some beautiful music, some chanting, a recording of birdsong or waves crashing against the shore. You could also play an instrument. If you can't play an instrument, use a Tibetan singing bowl, wind chimes or bells – anything that makes a pleasant or resonant sound.

STAGE 3

Now move on to awareness of touch. Ask your lover to be aware of the surfaces of their body, particularly those that are in contact with the ground. Can they feel any air moving against their skin? Are some parts of their body a different temperature from others? Tell them that you are going to place your fingertip on their lips but that you're not going to do it immediately. Wait 30 seconds to build up a sense of anticipation.

Slowly move your fingertip down their chin and neck and use it to draw circles and spirals on their chest and shoulders. Ask them to follow the path of your fingertip in their mind. Now, if you want to, you can move on to the touch meditation techniques. Otherwise, end this stage of the sensual awakening by wrapping your lover in a warm gown, shawl or blanket.

STAGE 4

Prepare a series of foods and drinks that you know will delight your lover: these might be a slice of mango or pineapple, a tiny chunk of dark chocolate, a sip of champagne, the tip of an asparagus spear, a lick of honey or cream. Keep the quantities of food and drink tiny and feed each treat to your lover one by one, leaving time between each one. Finish this stage of the sensual awakening by tenderly kissing your lover so that the last taste they have is of you.

STAGE 5

This is the end of the sensual awakening programme: slowly take your lover's blindfold off and ask them to look at you. Hold their gaze and look deeply into each other's eyes. Try to maintain this connection.

giving an energy massage

The aim of this massage is to stimulate your lover's energy body as well as their physical body and encourages energy to move upward. By the end of the massage they should feel tranquil, yet energized. Take some time to unwind and connect with each other – try doing an exercise such as the sensual awakening (see pages 116 – 17) to bring you into a mindful state.

STEP 1 (see above right) **Ask your lover to lie on their front, naked. Kneel beside them and hold your palms a short distance from the base of their spine. Close your eyes and start to visualize the energy emanating from their body.**

STEP 2 (see below right) **When you're ready, move your hands in circles above the point at the base of their spine. Then gradually move your hands in circular movements up your lover's spine (still not touching the skin). Imagine that you are touching your**

lover's "energy body" and moving energy up through the chakras (see page 110).

STEP 3 **When you get to your lover's neck (the site of the throat chakra), hold your hands still above the skin and ask your lover to breathe out any negative energy or feelings. It can help if they visualize exhaling negative energy in the form of dark, smoky or polluted air.**

STEP 4 (see far right) **Move your hands back down to the base of the spine. Now**

you're going to use your palms to make contact with your lover's skin. Rest both hands on the spot at the base of the spine. Circle your hands on this spot. Without taking your hands off your lover's body, slide them up to the sacral area and circle them again here.

STEP 5 **Repeat the circling motion from step 4 at the level of the solar plexus, heart and neck chakras. When you get to the neck chakra, once again ask your lover to visualize exhaling negative energy in the form of dark, smoky or polluted air.**

STEP 6 **Return your hands to the base of the spine and repeat the massage, this time applying deeper pressure with your palms.**

tantric massage for her

The aim of this massage is to reduce muscle tension in and around your lover's vagina. You will be massaging away tension that may have been stored there for many years. Your lover may become aroused during the massage, but your primary aim is to heal rather than to arouse.

It's important that your lover feels happy with everything you're doing. Ask your lover for plenty of feedback and encourage her to breathe deeply and make any kinds of noise she wants to throughout the massage. Ask her to tell you if you touch an area that feels tense or uncomfortable. If the area you touch is tense, keep massaging it until the tension starts to dissolve; if it's uncomfortable, stop the massage or try a different technique.

THE WARM-UP

Ask permission before you begin. Then, making sure that your finger is lubricated, gently move it in circles around the entrance to your lover's vagina. After a while, ask your lover if you can penetrate her with your finger. If she agrees, slide the tip of your finger (use two fingers if she wants you to) into her vagina.

RINGS OF TISSUE

Imagine that your lover's vagina consists of several rings or bands of tissue, one on top of the other. The first ring of tissue is just inside the entrance to her vagina; the last ring of tissue is high up in her vagina by the cervix. You are slowly and firmly going to massage each of these rings of tissue in turn – the exact technique you use isn't important. For example, you can use firm, static pressure with the tip of your finger or you can move your fingertip in circles. Ask your lover which stroke or strokes feel most effective and pleasurable.

THE G-SPOT

Tantric massage can also be effective on the front wall of the vagina – especially on the G-spot (see page 67). If you're not confident about locating this zone, ask your lover to help. Massaging this area for a prolonged period can be an intense experience for many women. Lots of tension due to unsatisfying or frustrating sexual experiences can get lodged here and deep massage can bring a profound sense of relief or "letting go", and intense sexual pleasure.

tantric massage for him

This massage relaxes and loosens the muscles around the penis and the scrotum. It releases genital armouring (see page 112), increases penile sensitivity and enhances sensation during sex.

Ask your lover for feedback throughout the massage to make sure he feels comfortable with everything you're doing. Encourage him to breathe deeply throughout.

THE WARM-UP

It's important that your hands are well lubricated for this massage, so use plenty of oil. Ask your lover to lie down in a comfortable position and start by stroking his abdomen and thighs. Move one hand so that your fingertips are resting on the muscles that lie just underneath his scrotum, at the junction between the thigh and the perineum. Use your other hand to lift up his testicles to give you easier access.

Apply gradual circular pressure along the junction between his thigh and perineum. Work your way down this junction. If you sense tension in a particular area, stop and work on it. Next, work on the junction between the opposite thigh and perineum.

PERINEAL MASSAGE

Now massage the perineum itself, pressing your fingertips in circular movements. Your aim is to release tension and free all the muscles in this area. Concentrate particularly on areas of tension that you sense, or which your lover alerts you to. Next massage the muscles at the base of your lover's penis. Use your fingers in whatever way comes most naturally to you – the exact technique you use isn't important.

ANAL MASSAGE

The last part of the massage is optional for both the giver and the receiver. It consists of massaging the anus with the aim of releasing muscle tension in this area. Move your well-lubricated fingers in circles around the anus, encouraging the muscles to relax and open up. Breathe deeply in and out in time with your lover. As his muscles begin to soften, slowly slide your finger into his anal entrance and stroke firmly. Slowly and gently push your fingers deeper into your lover. Stroke the front wall of the rectum and use your fingers to massage the P-spot (see page 69). Massage this sensitive place for as long as your lover wants you to.

cultivating erotic bliss

One of the aims of Tantric sex is to turn erotic pleasure from a solely genital experience into a whole-body experience. Orgasm, instead of being felt locally in the penis or the vagina and clitoris, becomes a vibration that can be felt from head to toe. By tuning into and harnessing sexual energy you can increase the eroticism of your love-making and enjoy new heights of pleasure.

SEXUAL ENERGY

A core part of Tantric theory is sexual energy. People usually dissipate their sexual energy by reaching orgasm fairly quickly – they do this through lots of intensive or fast genital stimulation in the form of intercourse, masturbation or oral sex.

Tantric sex teachers advocate a different approach: building up sexual energy slowly over a period of time and, instead of releasing it through orgasm, redirecting it internally up through a central chan-nel in the body. The following exercise combines sex and massage. It will help you to direct sexual energy internally, and experience erotic pleasure all over your body.

THE WARM-UP

Prepare your erotic space with candles and essential oils (see page 114). He sits cross-legged on the floor and she sits astride him (with her feet behind his body) so that his penis is near her vagina. Gaze deeply into each other's eyes. Press your foreheads together, close your eyes and enjoy the sense of connection that this brings. Massage each other's face and body with the tips of your fingers (don't touch the genitals yet – the point is to build up arousal slowly and steadily).

Imagine that your fingers and your lover's fingers are wands of light that can deliver the most ecstatic warm, glowing sensations. Breathe in time with each other and concentrate on all the delicious feelings that are coming into your body via your lover's fingertips. See if you can make each other's hairs stand on end.

FINGERTIP AROUSAL

Once you've spent 15 minutes massaging each other's face and body, move your fingers to your lover's buttocks and genitals. Instead of moving them in an intense, rhythmic way – as you would if trying to bring your lover to orgasm – just let your fingertips dance and play lightly and randomly all over your lover's genitals. As the two of you become aroused, she can gently guide his erect penis into her vagina.

BLISSFUL SEX

Once you are joined in intercourse, rather than thrusting or moving your bodies, make subtle internal movements by contracting and relaxing the muscles that surround the penis (see page 59) and vagina (see page 57). This not only massages and stimulates both of you, but also helps to draw up sexual energy inside your body.

Breathe in time with each other. Concentrate on all the sensual and erotic feelings in your genitals. Start to imagine that you are pulling these sensations up into your body as you inhale. Contract your sex muscles at the same time. Feel the sexual energy expanding into your belly as you do this – you may experience this feeling as a sense of warmth, light or tingling.

As you breathe out, let your sex muscles relax and allow the sexual energy to move back down into your genitals. Practise this as many times as you like – it may take several sessions before you begin to experience the sense of sexual energy moving up and down. If you find this difficult, practise moving your sex muscles in time with your breathing when you are not having sex. When you've got the hang of this, try it again during lovemaking.

DRAWING UP SEXUAL ENERGY

Once you are confident that you can draw sexual energy up toward your navel, try using the same techniques of muscle contraction and inhalation to draw sexual energy higher in your body – to your chest if you can (and then dropping it down again).

Imagine that there is a channel that runs from your perineum to the crown of your head. (This channel is widely recognized in Eastern traditions and is sometimes known as the Hollow Bamboo or the Inner Flute.) Practise drawing up energy through this channel to the level of your solar plexus, heart, throat, brow and, eventually, all of the way to the crown of your head. This is quite an advanced Tantric practice so make sure you take it a step at a time.

CARESSING BREATH

Try exploring the whole of your lover's body with your breath: include their toes, the soles of their feet, the sensitive places behind their knees, their fingertips and their eyelids. Experiment with different types of breath. Try breathing out slowly from your throat as if you were trying to steam up a window. Try pursing your lips and blowing out a fast stream of air. Try licking the surface of your lover's skin – or wetting it with an ice cube – and then blowing very softly on the moist skin. Sensual bliss...

loving breath

One of the aims of Tantric touch is to be at one with your lover, and there is no greater way to do this than by stimulating your lover's energy body using your breath alone. It is one of the subtlest and most sensual massage tools imaginable, creating a feeling that is simply sublime.

THE WARM-UP

Sit facing each other with your hands on your chest (this is the area of your heart chakra, which governs love, compassion and creativity). Look into each other's eyes and breathe deeply in synchrony with each other. Concentrate on the loving feelings that you have for your lover. Try silently repeating the words "I love you" as though it were a mantra. Sit close enough so that you can feel each other's exhalations gently mingling and caressing your faces. If your thoughts drift, return to focusing on the in-out movement of the breath.

BLOWING ENERGY ALONG THE BODY

Ask your lover to lie on their front. Sit or kneel beside them and breathe in deeply. As you exhale, gently blow across their buttocks in the direction of their head. Imagine that you are blowing your lover's energy up through the chakras. When your exhalation is complete, move so that you are sitting a little higher up their body, take another deep breath and blow out again in the direction of your lover's head. Keep doing this all the way up your lover's spine to their head.

Ask your lover to turn over on to their back. Now blow the energy back down their body: from the head, across the chest and belly and down to the genitals. Pause at the penis or vulva and caress these areas by gently blowing on them. Each time you breathe in, imagine that you are inhaling sexual energy from your lover's genitals. When you feel full of this sexual energy, blow it back up your lover's body in a line that comes to an end at their forehead.

KEEP PRACTISING

If you are not accustomed to Tantric practices, these subtle exercises may not yield much in terms of sensation in the beginning. But the more you practise them, the more profound they will feel and the greater the sensitivity you will develop in relation to one another.

Tantra is all about improving the sensual and sexual bond between you and there is no better way to do so than with this erotic bathtime treat. It can be mutual, where you take it in turns to pamper each other, or one person can be the giver and one the receiver. Take your lover by the hand and lead them to a hot, fragrant, candlelit bath. Instruct them not to speak but just to enjoy the sensual experience of being bathed. Carefully undress your lover and invite them to climb into the bath. Get in too if there's room; otherwise just kneel beside the bath. Cover your lover in soapsuds or shower gel and then slowly wash every part of their body.

Massage shampoo into their scalp by pressing your fingertips and thumbs in big, firm circles. Firmly massage their back, neck and shoulders using a loofah or abrasive mitten. Move the palms of your hands in slow, gentle circles across their belly and chest. Squeeze and pinch the large muscles of their calves and thighs as you wash their legs. Take their feet in your hands and wash each toe individually — pinch and massage it along its length with soapy fingers. Finally, wash their genitals using lots of gel as a lubricant and light, fingertip strokes.

Invite your lover to step out of the bath and wrap them in a warm towel. Dry any exposed parts of their body with another towel — touch them as gently as you would a child. Now get into bed together.

CHAPTER FIVE

SELF-TOUCH

No one knows the intimate contours and curves of

your body like you do – and now is the time to put that

knowledge to good use. Self-massage can play a variety

of roles in your daily life: it can relieve sexual tension, it

can teach you things about your sexual responses (things

you can then teach to your lover!) and it can give you

a unique opportunity to relax, lose your inhibitions and

enjoy the pleasures of the body.

rediscover your body

If you watch a child expressing an emotion such as joy, fear or anger, the chances are that they will make dramatic physical gestures – jumping for joy or lying down and kicking the ground in rage, for example. As adults we generally learn to stop expressing ourselves physically. We start living more in our minds and less in our bodies. As part of this process we may lose an awareness of the innate sensitivity, sensuality and responsiveness of the body. Even pleasurable physical acts such as sex may stimulate the genitals but leave the rest of the body relatively "untouched". Sensual and erotic pleasure can be experienced all over the body, but in order for this to happen you first need to re-awaken your body.

LOVING YOUR BODY

One of the biggest challenges for many people is accepting and loving their body as it is. It can be tempting to defer sensual or sexual satisfaction because you're not happy with your body. For example, you might think: "I'll let my lover massage me naked when I'm thinner" or "We'll get our sex life back on track, when I've started going to the gym." The following exercise is designed to help you accept your body as it is right now.

Take all your clothes off in the privacy of your bedroom and stand in front of a full-length mirror. Acknowledge any critical thoughts that pop into your mind. Now challenge those thoughts – is there a kinder, gentler way of thinking about and looking at your body? Can you describe yourself as curvy or voluptuous instead of fat, for example? Can you see your body as the positive living history of everything that has happened to you in life? Now try to make the mental leap of imagining that your body belongs to someone else. If this were the case, the chances are that you would judge it less harshly. Pay your body as many compliments as you can. Stroke different parts of your body and think about times when you have given or received sensual pleasure.

VISUALIZATION TECHNIQUES

This exercise uses a combination of visualization and touch to re-awaken your natural physical sensitivity. Choose an easily accessible and sensitive part of your body such as your hand or your foot and then try one or all of the following visualizations. If you're with your lover, take turns to read the instructions aloud to each other.

TECHNIQUE 1

Imagine that your hand or foot is near a gentle source of heat and it is becoming comfortably warm. Feel your hand or foot getting softer and expanding in the heat. Now imagine the boundaries of your foot or hand becoming indistinct or dissolving. Picture your foot or hand melting.

TECHNIQUE 2

Imagine that you are sitting in a room waiting for a hand or a foot massage. It is going to be the most skilled and blissful massage you have ever experienced. Let your hand or foot tingle in anticipation.

TECHNIQUE 3

Imagine that you have been wearing a plaster cast on your hand or your foot and it has just been cut off after many weeks. Relish the sensation of the air against your fingers or your toes. Wiggle your toes or bend and flex your fingers and feel the intense sensual pleasure. Imagine that you can experience sexual arousal in your hand or your foot. Rub your fingers or your toes together. Describe any sensations that come to mind.

TOUCH TECHNIQUES

Rest the tip of your index finger on your hand or your foot (if you have been concentrating on your hand, use the index finger of your free hand). Imagine that this finger is conducting sensual or erotic energy into your hand or your foot. Focus all of your awareness on the point of contact between the tip of your finger and your hand or your foot. Feel the spot gently tingling or pulsating with pleasure.

Now try gently moving your fingertip across your hand or your foot and dragging the pleasurable sensation with it. If you can do this, move your finger up your arm or leg and then over the rest of your body, stimulating, lighting up or energizing each bit.

DURING LOVEMAKING

Once you've managed to "eroticize" different parts of your body (it can take some practice to achieve this), try to repeat the experience during sex. When you feel aroused genitally, imagine moving these erotic sensations around your body – down your legs or through your belly up to your chest, for example. Try to make sex a whole-body experience.

secret pleasure zones

The whole body can be a source of sensual and erotic pleasure but there are some hot spots that feel especially wonderful when massaged. Touch yourself all over with oiled hands to discover your secret pleasure zones.

THE S-SPOT

This is a spot on the neck that was named by massage therapist Kenneth Ray Stubbs (the "S" stands for Stubbs), which when massaged can cause pleasurable sensations in the genital area. The location of the S-spot is on either side of the top of the spine, usually about an inch down from the base of the skull. Stubbs says: "You are likely to find the S-spot on a muscle that is tight, often like a very thin rope. To stimulate the spot, you twang the rope with the soft pads of your fingertips." You can massage your own S-spot using the index finger and middle finger of both hands.

AWAKENING THE DRAGON

In Eastern massage, stroking the inner and outer thighs is a way of treating sexual problems such as vaginismus and erection difficulties. It also feels incredibly sensual. Sit up with the soles of your feet pressed together and

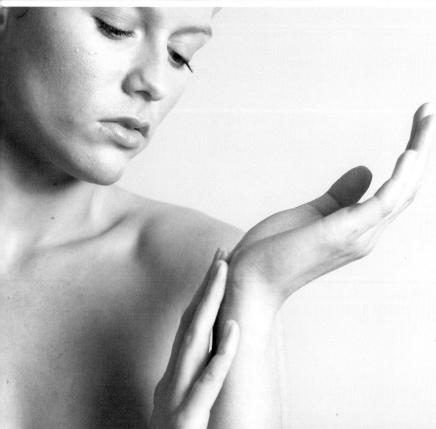

your knees falling out to the sides. You can also sit cross-legged. Place your palms on your knees and let them rest there for a few moments. Slowly and gently slide your hands up the insides of your thighs. When you get to the tops of your legs, move your fingertips along the crease of your groin, round to your hips. Now move your hands softly down the outsides of your thighs to your knees. Continue this circular stroke, gradually reducing the pressure until your hands are barely touching your skin.

THE WRISTS AND FINGERS

It's easy to neglect the wrists and hands when giving self massage but they are easy to access and can yield some exquisite sensations. Try this stroke: brush your wrist repeatedly with the flats of your fingernails – do this incredibly lightly. Then drag your nails up across the palm of your hand and use your fingertip to trace around the outside of each finger. Pause when you get to the fingertip and imagine energy passing between your fingers. When you reach your little finger, trace a line down the outside of your hand and end up back at your wrist. Finish by rubbing your hands together very lightly so that the surfaces of your palms barely touch.

a massage for one

This lovely sensual massage will relax you and make you tingle from head to toe. Prepare for it as you would if you were massaging someone else: get your oils ready, make the room warm and pleasant, and make sure that your privacy is guaranteed.

STEP 1 (see left) **Undress and sit on the floor with your legs out in front of you. Bend one of your legs so that you can massage your foot. Coat your hands in oil and circle your thumbs on the top of your foot, covering the whole surface. Press your fingers into the sole of your foot applying firm, static pressure, covering the whole of the bottom of your foot. Take each toe between your thumb and forefinger and bend it backward and forward, and then tug and twist it.**

Now bend your knee and rest your foot on the calf of the opposite leg. Press both your hands flat on either side of your foot to make a sandwich. Feel your foot gradually becoming warm, supple and relaxed from the pressure of your hands. Now slowly slide your hands off your foot in the direction of your toes. Repeat this massage on the other foot.

STEP 2 **Lie on your back and take a few slow, deep breaths. Rest the palm of your hand on your belly and move it slowly in big clockwise circles. Note any sensations in your hand as you touch yourself. What does your belly feel like to your hand: soft or firm; warm or cool; rough or smooth? Don't make any critical**

judgements about your body; instead, simply observe. Now switch your awareness to the sensations in your belly. How does it feel to have your belly stroked: relaxing, stimulating or arousing? Are the sensations localized or do they radiate to your stomach or genitals or somewhere else?

STEP 3 **Now repeat step 2 and see if you can switch your awareness back and forth between the sensations in your hand and the sensations in your belly. This takes practice and you may find that all the various sensations merge into one at first.**

Even if you find it difficult, this is a worthwhile practice because it encourages you to concentrate on bodily sensations and stops you being distracted.

STEP 4 (see previous page) **Let your knees drop to one side, but keep your shoulders flat on the floor so that you are lying in a twist. Use the hand nearest your raised buttock to firmly massage the large buttock muscle – make your middle fingers and forefingers as stiff as you can and walk them backward and forward across the muscle, pressing fairly hard as you do so. If you come across any points of tension, stop and press your fingers deeply into the muscle. Visualize the muscle fibres becoming warm and soft in response to your touch.**

STEP 5 **Relax your fingers and use your fingertips, fingernails or the backs of your fingers to lightly caress and graze the skin. Now position yourself in a twist (see step 4) on the other side of your body and repeat the massage on the other buttock.**

STEP 6 **Draw your knees up to your chest and hug them in your arms. Let your body become as heavy as possible – imagine it sinking into the floor. With your eyes closed, roll very slowly from side to side so that the floor massages the large muscles in your back. Roll your head from side to side too.**

STEP 7 **Return to lying flat on the floor and allow yourself a long, languorous stretch. Then wrap your arms around your chest and tuck each palm into the opposite armpit. Slowly slide your hands back across your chest so that they cross paths in the middle (women can slide their hands directly across their breasts or with one hand above the breasts and one hand below – whichever feels most comfortable).**

When your hands reach your sides, slide them back again. Keep repeating this but gradually start to lessen the amount of pressure you apply, until you are using the lightest of feathery touches.

STEP 8 (see right) **Still using a featherlight touch, let your fingertips travel from your chest along the length of your neck and over your jawbone and chin so that they come to rest on your lips. Delicately trace the line of your lips – touch the sensitive place just inside (imagine you are applying lip balm to the moist tissue just inside your mouth).**

As you did with your belly and your hand in step 3, try to differentiate between the sensations in your lips and those in your fingertips. Use your fingers to trace the contours of your face and neck.

STEP 9 **Gently rest your middle three fingertips on the inner part of each eyebrow or** slightly above. Draw your hands apart so that your fingers come to rest on your temples. Circle your fingers firmly on your temples several times and then repeat the stroke across your eyebrows.

Finally, rake all your fingers through your hair, pressing on your scalp as you go – start some of the strokes from the nape of the neck and some from the hairline at the top of your head.

STEP 10 **End the massage by making long, sweeping strokes down the length of your whole body. Relax and let your hands glide all the way from your chest to your legs.**

If you want to move on to erotic self-massage now, place your palm on your genitals and keep it completely still for a few moments. Again relax, and savour the feeling of warmth and pressure.

sexual self-touch for her

Close the door to your bedroom and devote some time to pure self-eroticism. Prepare the room as you might for a lover, making sure your privacy is guaranteed and that you have plenty of time.

THE WARM-UP

Make yourself comfortable, close your eyes and drift off into a favourite fantasy. Allow a warm, erotic glow to build up inside your body. Let your hands play on your skin: skim the surface of your neck, chest and nipples with your fingertips, or gently drag your nails across your belly.

GENITAL CARESS

Now get a small mirror, open your legs and look at your genitals. Enjoy the sensuality of looking at this body part that is normally hidden from view. Gently touch different places and imagine that you are trying to rate each place for sensitivity. Now start to caress the parts that feel most sensitive. Rather than rushing to reach orgasm, slowly explore your genitals. If you're accustomed to masturbating with one or two fingers, use three or four – or use the palm or heel of your hand – instead. If you normally use a circular stroke, try a backward and forward or a side-to-side stroke.

BE EXPERIMENTAL

Whatever you do usually, try something different. Instead of using your fingers, squeeze your thighs together rhythmically or try touching yourself with props such as a feather. Move however you want to and make as much noise you want to as you bring yourself to climax.

THE EROTIC THREAD

Imagine that your clitoris, vagina and nipples are connected by a thread. As you stroke your nipples, feel the erotic charge that travels down the thread and switches on your genitals. Now move your hand to your clitoris – as you stimulate yourself, imagine the erotic charge zipping back along the thread to your vagina and nipples. Stroke your nipples and clitoris simultaneously and imagine eroticism moving up and down the thread like electricity. As the sexual tension builds, imagine the thread getting tauter and tighter.

sexual self-touch for him

Instead of masturbating quickly, using the strokes you always use, take time to treat yourself to a languorous and sensual experience. Let your body move in whatever way comes naturally. Make however much noise you want to. Pick a time when you know that you'll have complete privacy.

THE WARM-UP

Cover your hands in oil and stroke your inner thighs. Bypass your balls and penis and stroke your belly. Slide your hands back down your thighs. Breathe in and, as you breathe out, feel any tension flow out of your body. Close your eyes and visualize your ideal lover sitting astride you stroking you with her hands. Imagine how she would touch your penis. Would she use a soft or a hard touch? Would it be fast or slow? Take your penis in your hand and emulate the strokes you're fantasizing about.

BE EXPERIMENTAL

Even when you feel aroused, rather than touching yourself in a habitual way, be experimental. For example, place your palms on either side of the shaft of your penis and rub them backward and forward (as if you were rubbing sticks together to make fire). From this stroke you can interlock your fingers around your shaft and use both hands to stroke your penis up and down. Rather than lying on your back, try squatting against a wall or kneeling with the heel of one foot pressed against your perineum.

You're in no rush to ejaculate so, if you feel close to coming, just decrease the speed or the pressure of the stroke you are using, or use your hands to massage your thighs, chest or belly instead of your penis. When you do feel ready to climax, give yourself up to the experience.

STAYING POWER

Massaging your penis is a good way of becoming intimately acquainted with the point of no return – the point at which there is nothing you can do to stop yourself coming. The technical name for this is ejaculatory inevitability. When you sense you are approaching this point, stop stimulating your penis and let your arousal levels go down a couple of notches. Do this several times. Once you've learned ejaculatory control during masturbation, you can apply it during sex – which means you can last as long as you want to!

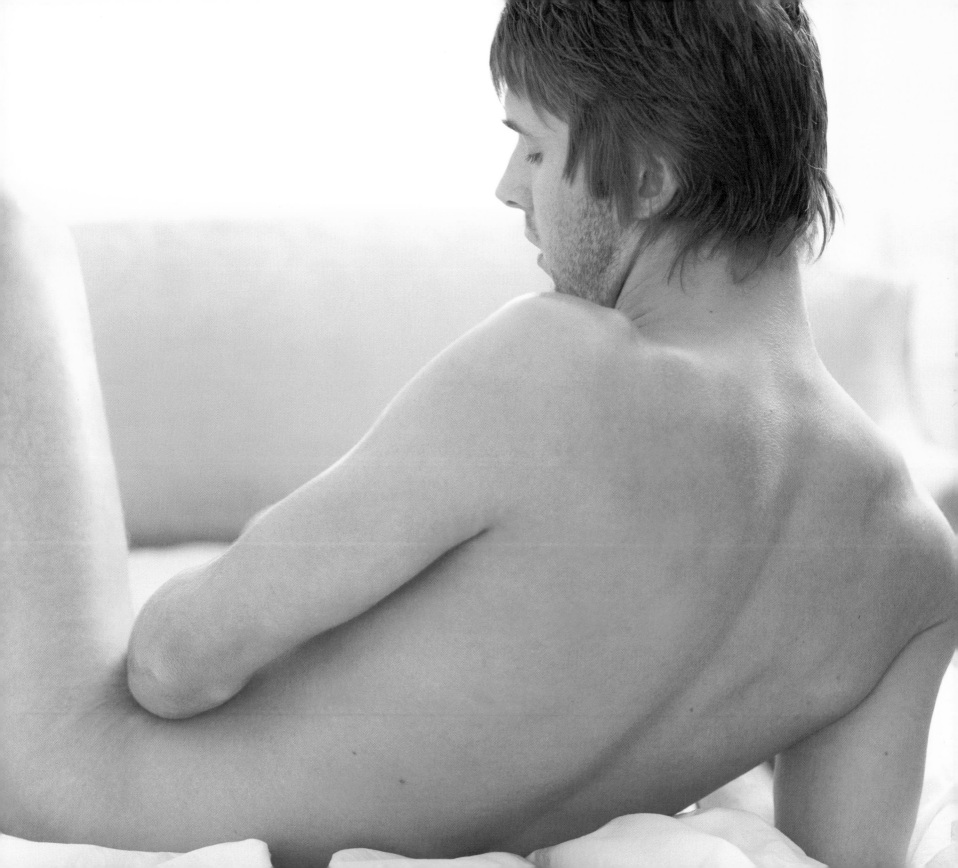

watching each other

Watching your lover give themselves an erotic massage is both sexy and educational. As the watcher you learn what kind of touch your lover enjoys most – and it's almost inevitable that you'll get turned on during the viewing process! Watching each other is also a great way to build trust: you're effectively saying to your lover that you feel safe enough in their presence to let go and abandon yourself to pure pleasure.

WHEN YOU'RE BEING WATCHED

Lie back on the bed and touch your body in whatever way comes naturally to you. You can start by stroking your arms, legs or feet to get into a relaxed sensual mood (see the sensual self-massage on pages 136–9). Or you can stimulate your penis or clitoris straight away if you want to – you're in charge. If you feel self-conscious, do whatever makes you feel relaxed: try closing your eyes and imagining you are alone. Alternatively, meet your lover's gaze for reassurance. If you feel like it, lie close to your lover so that you can sense their arousal. When you feel turned on, express it: writhe, thrust, moan, cry out. Trust your lover enough to let yourself go completely.

WHEN YOU'RE THE WATCHER

Don't do this exercise if there's any possibility that you might laugh, judge or criticize your lover (even silently). Reassure your lover in advance that you'll watch in a spirit of love. Because this exercise is primarily about letting your lover express themselves sexually in an atmosphere of trust, don't let your own arousal take over and dominate. Watch your lover to see which areas of their body they pay most attention to and what kind of speed, pressure and type of touch they use on themselves.

THE VOYEUR AND THE EXHIBITIONIST

If you're already at ease with and accustomed to watching each other, turn this exercise into a role-playing game. One of you plays the exhibitionist, while the other is the voyeur. As the exhibitionist, your role is to tease your lover by stimulating and caressing your body, but forbidding them from touching you. You can dress in a sexy costume or be entirely naked. Your voyeuristic lover, on the other hand, must remain dressed throughout and is not allowed to touch either themselves or you.

The great thing about sensual self-pleasure is that it can be enjoyed at any time – you just need yourself, your hand and a little imagination! So take time out to indulge. Lie down somewhere where you can relax and won't be disturbed. Close your eyes and let all your facial muscles relax: the area around your eyes and your cheeks, your mouth and, in particular, your jaw. Mentally scan your body for pockets of tension: when you sense tension, inhale, and imagine that your breath is going directly to that area. As you exhale, let the tension leave your body along with your breath.

When your entire body feels relaxed and receptive, stroke your body – you can do this through your clothes if it's easier. Don't worry about giving yourself a formal massage – take your time and concentrate on simple stroking movements. Allow your hands to intuitively change the amount of pressure that they apply as they move over different surfaces of your body. You'll find that you want to touch some parts of your body lightly with your fingertips and press other parts hard with your palms. Now you are immersed in bodily sensation, focus your attention on your genitals and the erotic charge within them. Rest your hand on your genitals and imagine drawing up erotic energy into your body with each breath. Visualize this energy as red, and imagine it permeating your whole body. Enjoy the sensuality of this for as long as you like.

further reading

Anand, Margot *The New Art of Sexual Ecstasy* (Thorsons, 2003)

Bentley, Eilean *The Essential Massage Book* (Gaia Books, 2005)

Davis, Patricia *Aromatherapy, an A-Z* (Vermillion, 2005)

Hooper, Anne *Pure Sex* (Duncan Baird Publishers, 2003)

Friday, Nancy *Women on Top* (Arrow, 1993)

Inkeles, Gordon *The New Sensual Massage* (Arcata Arts, 1998)

Lorius, Cassandra *101 Nights of Tantric Sex* (Thorsons, 2002)

Mehta, Narendra *Indian Head Massage* (HarperCollins, 2000)

O'Keefe, Adele *Official Guide to Body Massage* (Thomson Learning Vocational, 2006)

Stubbs, Kenneth Ray *Erotic Passions* (Secret Garden Publishing, 2000)

Stanway, Andrew *Massage Secrets for Lovers* (Quadrille Publishing 2002)

Winks, Cathy *The Good Vibrations Guide: The G-spot* (Down There Press, 1999)

index

Author's acknowledgments
Thanks to Grace Cheetham, Manisha Patel, Jantje Doughty and Dawn Bates at Duncan Baird.

Publisher's acknowledgments
The publishers would like to thank:
Photography: John Davis (represented by Gina Phillips)
Photographic assistants: Danny Graff, Steve Pound and Dave Foster
Make up artists: Nadine Wilkie, Stephen McIlmoyle and Britta D
Models: supplied by International Models Management (IMM), London